The Virgin Martyr by Philip Massinger

Written with Thomas Dekker

Philip Massinger was baptized at St. Thomas's in Salisbury on November 24th, 1583.

Massinger is described in his matriculation entry at St. Alban Hall, Oxford (1602), as the son of a gentleman. His father, who had also been educated there, was a member of parliament, and attached to the household of Henry Herbert, 2nd Earl of Pembroke. The Earl was later seen as a potential patron for Massinger.

He left Oxford in 1606 without a degree. His father had died in 1603, and accounts suggest that Massinger was left with no financial support this, together with rumours that he had converted to Catholicism, meant the next stage of his career needed to provide an income.

Massinger went to London to make his living as a dramatist, but he is only recorded as author some fifteen years later, when The Virgin Martyr (1621) is given as the work of Massinger and Thomas Dekker.

During those early years as a playwright he wrote for the Elizabethan stage entrepreneur, Philip Henslowe. It was a difficult existence. Poverty was always close and there was constant pleading for advance payments on forthcoming works merely to survive.

After Henslowe died in 1616 Massinger and John Fletcher began to write primarily for the King's Men and Massinger would write regularly for them until his death.

The tone of the dedications in later plays suggests evidence of his continued poverty. In the preface of The Maid of Honour (1632) he wrote, addressing Sir Francis Foljambe and Sir Thomas Bland: "I had not to this time subsisted, but that I was supported by your frequent courtesies and favours."

The prologue to The Guardian (1633) refers to two unsuccessful plays and two years of silence, when the author feared he had lost popular favour although, from the little evidence that survives, it also seems he had involved some of his plays with political characters which would have cast shadows upon England's alliances.

Philip Massinger died suddenly at his house near the Globe Theatre on March 17th, 1640. He was buried the next day in the churchyard of St. Saviour's, Southwark, on March 18th, 1640. In the entry in the parish register he is described as a "stranger," which, however, implies nothing more than that he belonged to another parish.

Index of Contents

INTRODUCTION

This very beautiful play, one of Massinger's earliest and most popular works, was first printed in 1622, but we have no account when it was first produced. In the composition of it he was assisted by Decker, a dramatist of no mean reputation.

The plot of this tragedy is founded on the tenth and last general persecution of the Christians, which broke out in the nineteenth year of Dioclesian's reign with a fury hard to be expressed; the Christians being every where, without distinction of age, sex, or condition, dragged to execution, and subjected to the most exquisite torments that rage, cruelty, and hatred could suggest.

In the construction of their play, Massinger and his associate Decker appear to have conceived the idea of combining the prominent parts of the old Mystery with the Morality, which was not yet obliterated from the memories, nor perhaps from the affections, of many of the spectators. Among the many instances of skill displayed by the authors of The Virgin-Martyr in the management of their materials may be remarked the dexterity and good taste with which they have avoided the untimely concurrence of the good and evil spirit; an error into which Tasso and others of greater name than Massinger have inadvertently fallen.—Of the character of the heroine it is impossible to speak too highly: her genuine and dignified piety, her unsullied innocence, her unshaken constancy, her lofty pity for her persecutors, her calm contempt of torture, and her heroic death, exalt the mind in no ordinary degree. All the other parts are subordinate to her, and require little observation. Antoninus is brave and generous, and we sympathize with his genuine attachment for Dorothea. Calista and Christeta, hasty, self-confident, readily promising for their steadiness, soon forgetting their resolutions, and equally secure in every change of opinion, are well contrasted with the heroine of the piece, whose fixed principles always guard her against rashness, and therefore preserve her from contradiction. Artemia's love for Antoninus would be wholly without interest, if we were not moved for a moment by her indignation at the rejection of her offer; and we see her at length consigned to Maximinus with as little emotion as is shown by themselves.

The introduction of a good and evil spirit disguised in human shapes was not to be expected in a work aspiring to the reputation of a regular tragedy: still, whatever be their departure from propriety, it must be remembered that such representations had a most solemn origin, and that the business in which the spirits are engaged has a substantial conformity with the opinions of the early ages in which the plot is laid. The opposition of the demons to the progress of the faith, and the reasoning and raillery which Dorothea expresses, under the influence of Angelo, against the pagan gods, are to be found in Justin, Tatian, Arnobius, and others. The separate agency of the spirits, and the consequence of their personal encounter, are also described in a characteristic manner.

Apart from Angelo, Harpax seems to advance in his malignant work. When the daughters of Theophilus express their zeal for paganism, he "grows fat to see his labours prosper;" yet he cannot look forward to the defeat of those labours in their approaching conversion, though on some occasions we find he could "see a thousand leagues" in his master's service. And this agrees with the doctrine, that when some signal triumph of the faith was at hand, the evil spirits were abridged of their usual powers. Again, when Harpax expects to meet Angelo, he thus expresses the dread of his presence, and the effect which it afterwards produced on him:

"—I do so hate his sight,
That, should I look on him, I should sink down."
Act II. Sc. 2.

And this, too, perfectly agrees with the power attributed to the superior spirits of quelling the demons by those indications of their quality which were not to be perceived by mortals: per occultissimæ signa præsentiæ, quæ angelicis sensibus etiam malignorum spirituum, potius quam infirmitati hominum, possunt esse perspicua. Civ. Dei, lib. ix.

The tragedy is too full of horrors; but this is a fault of which our ancestors were very tolerant.

DRAMATIS PERSONÆ

DIOCLESIAN,   }
MAXIMINUS,   } Emperors of Rome.
KING OF PONTUS.
KING OF EPIRE.
KING OF MACEDON.
SAPRITIUS, Governor of Cæsarea.
THEOPHILUS, a zealous persecutor of the Christians.
SEMPRONIUS, captain of SAPRITIUS' guards.
ANTONINUS, son to SAPRITIUS.
MACRINUS, friend to ANTONINUS.
HARPAX, an evil spirit, following THEOPHILUS in the shape
of a secretary.
ANGELO, a good spirit, serving DOROTHEA in the habit of a page.
JULIANUS,   }
GETA,   } servants of THEOPHILUS.
PRIEST OF JUPITER.
BRITISH SLAVE.

ARTEMIA, daughter to DIOCLESIAN.
CALISTA,   }

CHRISTETA,   } daughters to THEOPHILUS.
DOROTHEA, the Virgin-Martyr.

Officers and Executioners.

SCENE - Cæsarea.

THE VIRGIN-MARTYR

ACT I

SCENE I

The Governor's Palace.

Enter **THEOPHILUS** and **HARPAX**.

THEOPHILUS
Come to Cæsarea to-night!

HARPAX
Most true, sir.

THEOPHILUS
The emperor in person!

HARPAX
Do I live?

THEOPHILUS
'Tis wondrous strange! The marches of great princes,
Like to the motions of prodigious meteors,
Are step by step observed; and loud-tongued Fame
The harbinger to prepare their entertainment:
And, were it possible so great an army,
Though cover'd with the night, could be so near,
The governor cannot be so unfriended
Among the many that attend his person,
But, by some secret means, he should have notice
Of Cæsar's purpose;—in this, then, excuse me,
If I appear incredulous.

HARPAX
At your pleasure.

THEOPHILUS
Yet, when I call to mind you never fail'd me
In things more difficult, but have discover'd
Deeds that were done thousand leagues distant from me,
When neither woods, nor caves, nor secret vaults,
No, nor the Power they serve, could keep these Christians
Or from my reach or punishment, but thy magic
Still laid them open; I begin again
To be as confident as heretofore;
It is not possible thy powerful art
Should meet a check, or fail.

[Enter the **PRIEST** of Jupiter, bearing an Image, and followed by **CALISTA** and **CHRISTETA**.

HARPAX
Look on the Vestals,
The holy pledges that the gods have given you,
Your chaste, fair daughters. Were 't not to upbraid
A service to a master not unthankful,
I could say these, in spite of your prevention,
Seduced by an imagined faith, not reason,
(Which is the strength of nature) quite forsaking
The Gentile gods, had yielded up themselves
To this new-found religion. This I cross'd,
Discover'd their intents, taught you to use,
With gentle words and mild persuasions,
The power and the authority of a father,
Set off with cruel threats; and so reclaim'd them:
And, whereas they with torment should have died,
(Hell's furies to me, had they undergone it!)
[Aside.
They are now votaries in great Jupiter's temple,
And, by his priest instructed, grown familiar
With all the mysteries, nay, the most abstruse ones,
Belonging to his deity.

THEOPHILUS
'Twas a benefit,
For which I ever owe you.—Hail, Jove's flamen!
Have these my daughters reconciled themselves,
Abandoning for ever the Christian way,
To your opinion?

PRIEST
And are constant in it.
They teach their teachers with their depth of judgment,
And are with arguments able to convert

The enemies to our gods, and answer all
They can object against us.

THEOPHILUS
My dear daughters!

CALISTA
We dare dispute against this new-sprung sect,
In private or in public.

HARPAX
My best lady,
Perséver[1] in it.

CHRISTETA
And what we maintain, We will seal with our bloods.

HARPAX
Brave resolution!
I e'en grow fat to see my labours prosper.

THEOPHILUS
I young again. To your devotions.

HARPAX
Do—
My prayers be present with you.

[Exeunt **PRIEST, CALISTA**. and **CHRISTETA**.

THEOPHILUS
O my Harpax!
Thou engine of my wishes, thou that steel'st
My bloody resolutions, thou that arm'st
My eyes 'gainst womanish tears and soft compassion,
Instructing me, without a sigh, to look on
Babes torn by violence from their mothers' breasts
To feed the fire, and with them make one flame;
Old men, as beasts, in beasts' skins torn by dogs;
Virgins and matrons tire the executioners;
Yet I, unsatisfied, think their torments easy—

HARPAX
And in that, just, not cruel.

THEOPHILUS
Were all sceptres
That grace the hands of kings made into one,

And offer'd me, all crowns laid at my feet,
I would contemn them all,—thus spit at them;
So I to all posterities might be call'd
The strongest champion of the Pagan gods,
And rooter out of Christians.

HARPAX
Oh, mine own,
Mine own dear lord! to further this great work,
I ever live thy slave.

[Enter **SAPRITIUS** and **SEMPRONIUS**.

THEOPHILUS
No more—The governor.

SAPRITIUS
Keep the ports close[2], and let the guards be doubled;
Disarm the Christians; call it death in any
To wear a sword, or in his house to have one.

SEMPRONIUS
I shall be careful, sir.

SAPRITIUS
'Twill well become you.
Such as refuse to offer sacrifice
To any of our gods, put to the torture.
Grub up this growing mischief by the roots;
And know, when we are merciful to them,
We to ourselves are cruel.

SEMPRONIUS
You pour oil
On fire that burns already at the height:
I know the emperor's edict, and my charge,
And they shall find no favour.

THEOPHILUS
My good lord,
This care is timely for the entertainment
Of our great master, who this night in person
Comes here to thank you.

SAPRITIUS
Who! the emperor?

HARPAX

To clear your doubts, he doth return in triumph,
Kings lackeying[3] by his triumphant chariot;
And in this glorious victory, my lord,
You have an ample share: for know, your son,
The ne'er-enough commended Antoninus,
So well hath flesh'd his maiden sword[4], and dyed
His snowy plumes so deep in enemies' blood,
That, besides public grace beyond his hopes,
There are rewards propounded.

SAPRITIUS
I would know
No mean in thine, could this be true.

HARPAX
My head
Answer the forfeit.

SAPRITIUS
Of his victory
There was some rumour: but it was assured,
The army pass'd a full day's journey higher
Into the country.

HARPAX
It was so determined;
But, for the further honour of your son,
And to observe the government of the city,
And with what rigour, or remiss indulgence,
The Christians are pursued, he makes his stay here:

[Trumpets.

For proof, his trumpets speak his near arrival.

SAPRITIUS
Haste, good Sempronius, draw up our guards,
And with all ceremonious pomp receive
The conquering army. Let our garrison speak
Their welcome in loud shouts, the city show
Her state and wealth.

SEMPRONIUS
I'm gone.

[Exit.

SAPRITIUS

O, I am ravish'd
With this great honour! cherish, good Theophilus,
This knowing scholar. Send for your fair daughters;
I will present them to the emperor,
And in their sweet conversion, as a mirror,
Express your zeal and duty.

THEOPHILUS
Fetch them, good Harpax.

[Exit **HARPAX**.

[Enter **SEMPRONIUS**, at the head of the guard, soldiers leading three kings bound; **ANTONINUS** and
MACRINUS bearing the emperor's eagles; **DIOCLESIAN** with a gilt laurel on his head, leading in
ARTEMIA: **SAPRITIUS** kisses the emperor's hand, then embraces his son; **HARPAX** brings in **CALISTA** and
CHRISTETA. Loud shouts.

DIOCLESIAN
So: at all parts I find Cæsarea
Completely govern'd: the licentious soldier
Confined in modest limits, and the people
Taught to obey, and not compell'd with rigour:
The ancient Roman discipline revived,
Which raised Rome to her greatness, and proclaim'd her
The glorious mistress of the conquer'd world;
But, above all, the service of the gods,
So zealously observed, that, good Sapritius,
In words to thank you for your care and duty,
Were much unworthy Dioclesian's honour,
Or his magnificence to his loyal servants.—
But I shall find a time with noble titles
To recompense your merits.

SAPRITIUS
Mightiest Cæsar,
[5]Whose power upon this globe of earth is equal
To Jove's in heaven; whose victorious triumphs
On proud rebellious kings that stir against it,
Are perfect figures of his immortal trophies
Won in the Giants' war; whose conquering sword,
Guided by his strong arm, as deadly kills
As did his thunder! all that I have done,
Or, if my strength were centupled, could do,
Comes short of what my loyalty must challenge.
But, if in any thing I have deserved
Great Cæsar's smile, 'tis in my humble care
Still to preserve the honour of those gods,
That make him what he is: my zeal to them

I ever have express'd in my fell hate
Against the Christian sect that, with one blow,
(Ascribing all things to an unknown Power,)
Would strike down all their temples, and allows them
Nor sacrifice nor altars.

DIOCLESIAN
Thou, in this,
Walk'st hand in hand with me: my will and power
Shall not alone confirm, but honour all
That are in this most forward.

SAPRITIUS
Sacred Cæsar,
If your imperial majesty stand pleased
To shower your favours upon such as are
The boldest champions of our religion,
Look on this reverend man,

[Points to **THEOPHILUS**]

—to whom the power
Of searching out, and punishing such delinquents,
Was by your choice committed; and, for proof,
He hath deserved the grace imposed upon him,
And with a fair and even hand proceeded,
Partial to none, not to himself, or those
Of equal nearness to himself; behold
This pair of virgins.

DIOCLESIAN
What are these?

SAPRITIUS
His daughters.

ARTEMIA
Now by your sacred fortune, they are fair ones,
Exceeding fair ones: would 'twere in my power
To make them mine!

THEOPHILUS
They are the gods', great lady,
They were most happy in your service else:
On these, when they fell from their father's faith,
I used a judge's power, entreaties failing
(They being seduced) to win them to adore
The holy Powers we worship; I put on

The scarlet robe of bold authority,
And, as they had been strangers to my blood,
Presented them in the most horrid form,
All kind of tortures; part of which they suffer'd
With Roman constancy.

ARTEMIA
And could you endure,
Being a father, to behold their limbs
Extended on the rack?

THEOPHILUS
I did; but must
Confess there was a strange contention in me,
Between the impartial office of a judge,
And pity of a father; to help justice
Religion stept in, under which odds
Compassion fell:—yet still I was a father.
For e'en then, when the flinty hangman's whips
Were worn with stripes spent on their tender limbs,
I kneel'd, and wept, and begg'd them, though they would
Be cruel to themselves, they would take pity
On my gray hairs; now note a sudden change,
Which I with joy remember; those, whom torture,
Nor fear of death could terrify, were o'ercome
By seeing of my sufferings; and so won,
Returning to the faith that they were born in,
I gave them to the gods. And be assured
I that used justice with a rigorous hand,
Upon such beauteous virgins, and mine own,
Will use no favour, where the cause commands me,
To any other; but, as rocks, be deaf
To all entreaties.

DIOCLESIAN
Thou deserv'st thy place;
Still hold it, and with honour. Things thus order'd
Touching the gods, 'tis lawful to descend
To human cares, and exercise that power
Heaven has conferr'd upon me;—which that you,
Rebels and traitors to the power of Rome,
Should not with all extremities undergo,
What can you urge to qualify your crimes,
Or mitigate my anger?

KING of EPIRE [6]
We are now
Slaves to thy power, that yesterday were kings,

And had command o'er others; we confess
Our grandsires paid yours tribute, yet left us,
As their forefathers had, desire of freedom.
And, if you Romans hold it glorious honour,
Not only to defend what is your own,
But to enlarge your empire, (though our fortune
Denies that happiness,) who can accuse
The famish'd mouth, if it attempt to feed?
Or such, whose fetters eat into their freedoms,
If they desire to shake them off?

KING of PONTUS
We stand
The last examples, to prove how uncertain
All human happiness is; and are prepared
To endure the worst.

KING of MACEDON
That spoke, which now is highest
In Fortune's wheel, must, when she turns it next,
Decline as low as we are. This consider'd
Taught the Ægyptian Hercules, Sesostris,
That had his chariot drawn by captive kings,
To free them from that slavery;—but to hope
Such mercy from a Roman were mere madness:
We are familiar with what cruelty
Rome, since her infant greatness, ever used
Such as   she triumph'd over; age nor sex
Exempted from her tyranny; scepter'd princes
Kept in her common dungeons, and their children,
In scorn train'd up in base mechanic arts,
For public bondmen. In the catalogue
Of those unfortunate men, we expect to have
Our names remember'd.

DIOCLESIAN
In all growing empires,
Even cruelty is useful; some must suffer,
And be set up examples to strike terror
In others, though far off: but, when a state
Is raised to her perfection, and her bases
Too firm to shrink, or yield, we may use mercy,
And do 't with safety[7]: but to whom? not cowards,
Or such whose baseness shames the conqueror,
And robs him of his victory, as weak Perseus
Did great Æmilius[8]. Know, therefore, kings
Of Epire, Pontus, and of Macedon,
That I with courtesy can use my prisoners,

As well as make them mine by force, provided
That they are noble enemies: such I found you,
Before I made you mine; and, since you were so,
You have not lost the courages of princes,
Although the fortune. Had you born yourselves
Dejectedly, and base, no slavery
Had been too easy for you: but such is
The power of noble valour, that we love it
Even in our enemies, and taken with it,
Desire to make them friends, as I will you.

KING of EPIRE
Mock us not, Cæsar.

DIOCLESIAN
By the gods, I do not.
Unloose their bonds:—I now as friends embrace you.
Give them their crowns again.

KING of PONTUS
We are twice o'ercome;
By courage, and by courtesy.

KING of MACEDON
But this latter
Shall teach us to live ever faithful vassals
To Dioclesian, and the power of Rome.

KING of EPIRE
All kingdoms fall before her!

KING of PONTUS
And all kings
Contend to honour Cæsar!

DIOCLESIAN
I believe
Your tongues are the true trumpets of your hearts,
And in it I most happy. Queen of fate,
Imperious Fortune! mix some light disaster
With my so many joys, to season them,
And give them sweeter relish: I'm girt round
With true felicity; faithful subjects here,
Here bold commanders, here with new-made friends:
But, what's the crown of all, in thee, Artemia,
My only child, whose love to me and duty,
Strive to exceed each other!

ARTEMIA

I make payment
But of a debt, which I stand bound to tender
As a daughter and a subject.

DIOCLESIAN

Which requires yet
A retribution from me, Artemia,
Tied by a father's care, how to bestow
A jewel, of all things to me most precious:
Nor will I therefore longer keep thee from
The chief joys of creation, marriage rites;
Which that thou may'st with greater pleasures taste of,
Thou shalt not like with mine eyes, but thine own.
Among these kings, forgetting they were captives;
Or those, remembering not they are my subjects,
Make choice of any: By Jove's dreadful thunder,
My will shall rank with thine.

ARTEMIA

It is a bounty
The daughters of great princes seldom meet with;
For they, to make up breaches in the state,
Or for some other public ends, are forced
To match where they affect not[9]. May my life
Deserve this favour!

DIOCLESIAN

Speak; I long to know
The man thou wilt make happy.

ARTEMIA

If that titles,
Or the adored name of Queen could take me,
Here would I fix mine eyes, and look no further;
But these are baits to take a mean-born lady,
Not her that boldly may call Cæsar father:
In that I can bring honour unto any,
But from no king that lives receive addition:
To raise desert and virtue by my fortune,
Though in a low estate, were greater glory,
Than to mix greatness with a prince that owes[10]
No worth but that name only.

DIOCLESIAN

I commend thee;
'Tis like myself.

ARTEMIA

If, then, of men beneath me,
My choice is to be made, where shall I seek,
But among those that best deserve from you?
That have served you most faithfully; that in dangers
Have stood next to you; that have interposed
Their breasts as shields of proof, to dull the swords
Aim'd at your bosom; that have spent their blood
To crown your brows with laurel?

MACRINUS

Cytherea,
Great Queen of Love, be now propitious to me!

HARPAX [To **SAPRITIUS**]

Now mark what I foretold.

ANTONINUS

Her eye's on me.
Fair Venus' son, draw forth a leaden dart[11],
And, that she may hate me, transfix her with it;
Or, if thou needs wilt use a golden one,
Shoot it in the behalf of any other:
Thou know'st I am thy votary elsewhere. [Aside.

ARTEMIA [Advances to **ANTONINUS**]

Sir.

THEOPHILUS

How he blushes!

SAPRITIUS

Welcome, fool, thy fortune.
Stand like a block when such an angel courts thee!

ARTEMIA

I am no object to divert your eye
From the beholding.

ANTONINUS

Rather a bright sun,
Too glorious for him to gaze upon,
That took not first flight from the eagle's aerie.
As I look on the temples, or the gods,
And with that reverence, lady, I behold you,
And shall do ever.

ARTEMIA

And it will become you,
While thus we stand at distance; but, if love,
Love born out of the assurance of your virtues,
Teach me to stoop so low—

ANTONINUS
O, rather take A higher flight.

ARTEMIA
Why, fear you to be raised?
Say I put off the dreadful awe that waits
On majesty, or with you share my beams,
Nay, make you to outshine me; change the name
Of Subject into Lord, rob you of service
That's due from you to me, and in me make it
Duty to honour you, would you refuse me?

ANTONINUS
Refuse you, madam! such a worm as I am
Refuse what kings upon their knees would sue for!
Call it, great lady, by another name;
An humble modesty, that would not match
A molehill with Olympus.

ARTEMIA
He that's famous
For honourable actions in the war,
As you are, Antoninus, a proved soldier,
Is fellow to a king.

ANTONINUS
If you love valour,
As 'tis a kingly virtue, seek it out,
And cherish it in a king; there it shines brightest,
And yields the bravest lustre. Look on Epire,
A prince, in whom it is incorporate;
And let it not disgrace him that he was
O'ercome by Cæsar; it was victory,
To stand so long against him: had you seen him,
How in one bloody scene he did discharge
The parts of a commander and a soldier,
Wise in direction, bold in execution;
You would have said, Great Cæsar's self excepted,
The world yields not his equal.

ARTEMIA
Yet I have heard,
Encountering him alone in the head of his troop,

You took him prisoner.

KING of EPIRE
'Tis a truth, great princess:
I'll not detract from valour.

ANTONINUS
'Twas mere fortune;
Courage had no hand in it.

THEOPHILUS
Did ever man
Strive so against his own good?

SAPRITIUS
Spiritless villain!
How I am tortured! By the immortal gods,
I now could kill him.

DIOCLESIAN
Hold, Sapritius, hold,
On our displeasure, hold!

HARPAX
Why, this would make
A father mad; 'tis not to be endured;
Your honour's tainted in 't.

SAPRITIUS
By heaven, it is:
I shall think of it.

HARPAX
'Tis not to be forgotten.

ARTEMIA
Nay, kneel not, sir; I am no ravisher,
Nor so far gone in fond affection to you,
But that I can retire, my honour safe:—
Yet say, hereafter, that thou hast neglected
What, but seen in possession of another,
Will make thee mad with envy.

ANTONINUS
In her looks
Revenge is written.

MACRINUS

As you love your life,
Study to appease her.

ANTONINUS
Gracious madam, hear me.

ARTEMIA
And be again refused?

ANTONINUS
The tender of
My life, my service, or, since you vouchsafe it,
My love, my heart, my all: and pardon me,
Pardon, dread princess, that I made some scruple
To leave a valley of security,
To mount up to the hill of majesty,
On which, the nearer Jove, the nearer lightning.
What knew I, but your grace made trial of me;
Durst I presume to embrace, where but to touch
With an unmanner'd hand was death? The fox,
When he saw first the forest's king[12], the lion,
Was almost dead with fear; the second view
Only a little daunted him; the third,
He durst salute him boldly: pray you, apply this;
And you shall find a little time will teach me
To look with more familiar eyes upon you,
Than duty yet allows me.

SAPRITIUS
Well excused.

ARTEMIA
You may redeem all yet.

DIOCLESIAN
And, that he may
Have means and opportunity to do so,
Artemia, I leave you my substitute
In fair Cæsarea.

SAPRITIUS
And here, as yourself,
We will obey and serve her.

DIOCLESIAN
Antoninus,
So you prove hers, I wish no other heir;
Think on 't:—be careful of your charge, Theophilus;

Sapritius, be you my daughter's guardian.
Your company I wish, confederate princes,
In our Dalmatian wars: which finished
With victory I hope, and Maximinus,
Our brother and copartner in the empire,
At my request won to confirm as much,
The kingdoms I took from you we'll restore,
And make you greater than you were before.

[Exeunt all but **ANTONINUS** and **MACRINUS**.

ANTONINUS
Oh, I am lost for ever! lost, Macrinus!
The anchor of the wretched, hope, forsakes me,
And with one blast of Fortune all my light
Of happiness is put out.

MACRINUS
You are like to those
That are ill only, 'cause they are too well;
That, surfeiting in the excess of blessings,
Call their abundance want. What could you wish,
That is not fall'n upon you? honour, greatness,
Respect, wealth, favour, the whole world for a dower;
And with a princess, whose excelling form
Exceeds her fortune.

ANTONINUS
Yet poison still is poison,
Though drunk in gold; and all these flattering glories
To me, ready to starve, a painted banquet,
And no essential food. When I am scorch'd
With fire, can flames in any other quench me?
What is her love to me, greatness, or empire,
That am slave to another, who alone
Can give me ease or freedom?

MACRINUS
Sir, you point at
Your dotage on the scornful Dorothea:
Is she, though fair, the same day to be named
With best Artemia? In all their courses,
Wise men purpose their ends: with sweet Artemia,
There comes along pleasure, security,
Usher'd by all that in this life is precious:
With Dorothea (though her birth be noble,
The daughter to a senator of Rome,
By him left rich, yet with a private wealth,

And far inferior to yours) arrives
The emperor's frown, which, like a mortal plague,
Speaks death is near; the princess' heavy scorn,
Under which you will shrink; your father's fury,
Which to resist even piety forbids:—
And but remember that she stands suspected
A favourer of the Christian sect; she brings
Not danger, but assured destruction with her.
This truly weigh'd one smile of great Artemia
Is to be cherish'd, and preferr'd before
All joys in Dorothea: therefore leave her.

ANTONINUS
In what thou think'st thou art most wise, thou art
Grossly abused, Macrinus, and most foolish.
For any man to match above his rank,
Is but to sell his liberty. With Artemia
I still must live a servant; but enjoying
Divinest Dorothea, I shall rule,
Rule as becomes a husband: for the danger,
Or call it, if you will, assured destruction,
I slight it thus.—If, then, thou art my friend,
As I dare swear thou art, and wilt not take
A governor's place upon thee[13], be my helper.

MACRINUS
You know I dare, and will do any thing;
Put me unto the test.

ANTONINUS
Go, then, Macrinus,
To Dorothea; tell her I have worn,
In all the battles I have fought, her figure,
Her figure in my heart, which, like a deity,
Hath still protected me. Thou canst speak well;
And of thy choicest language spare a little,
To make her understand how much I love her,
And how I languish for her. Bear these jewels,
Sent in the way of sacrifice, not service,
As to my goddess: all lets[14] thrown behind me,
Or fears that may deter me, say, this morning
I mean to visit her by the name of friendship:—
No words to contradict this.

MACRINUS
I am yours:
And, if my travail this way be ill spent,
Judge not my readier will by the event.

[Exeunt.

FOOTNOTES:

[1] *Perséver.*] *So this word was anciently written and pronounced: thus the king, in Hamlet:*

—*but to perséver*
In obstinate condolement.
GIFFORD.

[2] *Sap. Keep the ports close.*] *This word, which is directly from the Latin, is so frequently used by Massinger and the writers of his time for the gates of a town, that it appears superfluous to produce any examples of it.—GIFFORD.*

[3] *Kings lackeying by his triumphant chariot.*] *Running by the side of it like lackeys or foot-boys.—* GIFFORD.

[4] *Flesh'd his maiden sword.*] *These words are from Shakspeare, of whose works Massinger appears to have been a great reader.*

[5] *Whose power, &c.*] *An imitation of the well-known line, Divisum imperium cum Jove Cæsar habet.—* GIFFORD.

[6] *K. of Epire. We are now*
Slaves to thy power, &c.]
I have observed several imitations of Massinger in the dramas of Mason: there is, for instance, a striking similarity between this spirited speech, and the indignant exclamation of the brave but unfortunate Caractacus:

—*"Soldier, I had arms,*
Had neighing steeds to whirl my iron cars,
Had wealth, dominions: dost thou wonder, Roman,
I fought to save them? What if Cæsar aims
To lord it universal o'er the world,
Shall the world tamely crouch to Cæsar's footstool?"
GIFFORD.

[7] *And do 't with safety.*] *This is admirably expressed: the maxim, however, though just, is of the most dangerous nature; for what ambitious chief will ever allow the state to be "raised to her perfection," or that the time for using "mercy with safety" is arrived? Even Dioclesian has his exceptions,—strong ones too! For Rome was old enough in his time. There is an allusion to Virgil, in the opening of this speech:*

Res dura, et novitas regni me talia cogunt
Moliri, &c.
GIFFORD.

[8] —as weak Perseus
Did great Æmilius.]
It is said that Perseus sent to desire Paulus Æmilius not to exhibit him as a spectacle to the Romans, and to spare him the indignity of being led in triumph. Æmilius replied coldly: The favour he asks of me is in his own power; he can procure it for himself.—COXETER.

[9] To match where they affect not.] This does better for modern than Roman practice; and, indeed, the author was thinking more of Hamlet than Dioclesian, in this part of the dialogue.—GIFFORD.

[10] Owes.] i. e. owns.

[11] Fair Venus' son, draw forth a leaden dart.] The idea of this double effect, to which Massinger has more than one allusion, is from Ovid:

Filius huic Veneris; figat tuus omnia, Phoebe,
Te meus arcus, ait:—Parnassi constitit arce,
Eque sagittifera promsit duo tela pharetra
Diversorum operum; fugat hoc, facit illud amorem.
Quod facit, auratum est, et cuspide fulget acuta;
Quod fugat, obtusum est, et habet sub arundine plumbum.
Met. lib. i. 470.

GIFFORD.

[12] —The fox,
When he saw first the forest's king, &c.]
The fable is from the Greek. In a preceding line there is an allusion to the proverb, Procul a Jove, sed procul a fulmine.—GIFFORD.

[13] A governor's place upon thee.] From the Latin: ne sis mihi tutor.—GIFFORD.

[14] —All lets.] i. e. All impediments.

ACT II

SCENE I

A Room in Dorothea's House.

Enter **DOROTHEA**, followed by **ANGELO** with a book and taper.

DOROTHEA
My book and taper.

ANGELO
Here, most holy mistress.

DOROTHEA

Thy voice sends forth such music, that I never
Was ravish'd with a more celestial sound.
Were every servant in the world like thee,
So full of goodness, angels would come down
To dwell with us: thy name is Angelo,
And like that name thou art; get thee to rest,
Thy youth with too much watching is opprest.

ANGELO

No, my dear lady, I could weary stars,
And force the wakeful moon to lose her eyes,
By my late watching, but to wait on you.
When at your prayers you kneel before the altar,
Methinks I'm singing with some quire in heaven,
So blest I hold me in your company:
Therefore, my most loved mistress, do not bid
Your boy, so serviceable, to get hence;
For then you break his heart.

DOROTHEA

Be nigh me still, then:
In golden letters down I'll set that day,
Which gave thee to me. Little did I hope
To meet such worlds of comfort in thyself,
This little, pretty body; when I, coming
Forth of the temple, heard my beggar-boy,
My sweet-faced, godly beggar-boy, crave an alms,
Which with glad hand I gave, with lucky hand!—
And, when I took thee home, my most chaste bosom,
Methought, was fill'd with no hot wanton fire,
But with a holy flame, mounting since higher,
On wings of cherubins, than it did before.

ANGELO

Proud am I, that my lady's modest eye
So likes so poor a servant.

DOROTHEA

I have offer'd
Handfuls of gold but to behold thy parents.
I would leave kingdoms, were I queen of some,
To dwell with thy good father; for, the son
Bewitching me so deeply with his presence,
He that begot him must do 't ten times more.
I pray thee, my sweet boy, show me thy parents;
Be not ashamed.

ANGELO
I am not: I did never
Know who my mother was; but, by yon palace,
Fill'd with bright heavenly courtiers, I dare assure you,
And pawn these eyes upon it, and this hand,
My father is in heaven: and, pretty mistress,
If your illustrious hour-glass spend his sand,
No worse than yet it does; upon my life,
You and I both shall meet my father there,
And he shall bid you welcome.

DOROTHEA
A blessed day!
We all long to be there, but lose the way.

[Exeunt.

SCENE II

A Street, Near Dorothea's House.

Enter **MACRINUS**, met by **THEOPHILUS** and **HARPAX**.

THEOPHILUS
The Sun, god of the day, guide thee, Macrinus!

MACRINUS
And thee, Theophilus!

THEOPHILUS
Glad'st thou in such scorn[1]?
I call my wish back.

MACRINUS
I'm in haste.

THEOPHILUS
One word,
Take the least hand[2] of time up:—stay.

MACRINUS
Be brief.

THEOPHILUS
As thought: I prithee tell me, good Macrinus,

How health and our fair princess lay together
This night, for you can tell; courtiers have flies[3],
That buzz all news unto them.

MACRINUS
She slept but ill.

THEOPHILUS
Double thy courtesy; how does Antoninus?

MACRINUS
Ill, well, straight, crooked,—I know not how.

THEOPHILUS
Once more;
—Thy head is full of windmills:—when doth the princess
Bestow herself on noble Antoninus?

MACRINUS
I know not.

THEOPHILUS
No! thou art the manuscript,
Where Antoninus writes down all his secrets:
Honest Macrinus, tell me.

MACRINUS
Fare you well, sir.

[Exit.

HARPAX
Honesty is some fiend, and frights him hence;
A many courtiers love it not.

THEOPHILUS
What piece
Of this state-wheel, which winds up Antoninus,
Is broke, it runs so jarringly? the man
Is from himself divided: O thou, the eye,
By which I wonders see, tell me, my Harpax,
What gad-fly tickles this Macrinus so,
That, flinging up the tail, he breaks thus from me.

HARPAX
Oh, sir, his brain-pan is a bed of snakes,
Whose stings shoot through his eye-balls, whose poisonous spawn
Ingenders such a fry of speckled villanies,

That, unless charms more strong than adamant
Be used, the Roman angel's[4] wings shall melt,
And Cæsar's diadem be from his head
Spurn'd by base feet; the laurel which he wears,
Returning victor, be enforced to kiss
That which it hates, the fire. And can this ram,
This Antoninus-Engine, being made ready
To so much mischief, keep a steady motion?—
His eyes and feet, you see, give strange assaults.

THEOPHILUS
I'm turn'd a marble statue at thy language,
Which printed is in such crabb'd characters,
It puzzles all my reading: what, in the name
Of Pluto, now is hatching?

HARPAX
This Macrinus,
The line is[5], upon which love-errands run
'Twixt Antoninus and that ghost of women,
The bloodless Dorothea; who in prayer
And meditation, mocking all your gods,
Drinks up her ruby colour: yet Antoninus
Plays the Endymion to this pale-faced Moon,
Courts, seeks to catch her eyes—

THEOPHILUS
And what of this?

HARPAX
These are but creeping billows,
Not got to shore yet: but if Dorothea
Fall on his bosom, and be fired with love,
(Your coldest women do so),—had you ink
Brew'd from the infernal Styx, not all that blackness
Can make a thing so foul, as the dishonours,
Disgraces, buffetings, and most base affronts
Upon the bright Artemia, star o' the court,
Great Cæsar's daughter.

THEOPHILUS
I now conster[6] thee.

HARPAX
Nay, more; a firmament of clouds, being fill'd
With Jove's artillery, shot down at once,
To pash[7] your gods in pieces, cannot give,
With all those thunderbolts, so deep a blow

To the religion there, and pagan lore,
As this; for Dorothea hates your gods,
And, if she once blast Antoninus' soul,
Making it foul like hers, Oh! the example—

THEOPHILUS
Eats through Cæsarea's heart like liquid poison.
Have I invented tortures to tear Christians,
To see but which, could all that feel hell's torments
Have leave to stand aloof here on earth's stage,
They would be mad till they again descended,
Holding the pains most horrid of such souls,
May-games to those of mine; has this my hand
Set down a Christian's execution
In such dire postures, that the very hangman
Fell at my foot dead, hearing but their figures;
And shall Macrinus and his fellow-masquer
Strangle me in a dance?

HARPAX
No:—on; I hug thee,
For drilling thy quick brains in this rich plot
Of tortures 'gainst these Christians: on; I hug thee!

THEOPHILUS
Both hug and holy me: to this Dorothea,
Fly thou and I in thunder.

HARPAX
Not for kingdoms
Piled upon kingdoms: there's a villain page
Waits on her, whom I would not for the world
Hold traffic with; I do so hate his sight,
That, should I look on him, I must sink down.

THEOPHILUS
I will not lose thee then, her to confound:
None but this head with glories shall be crown'd.

HARPAX
Oh! mine own as I would wish thee!

[Exeunt.

FOOTNOTES

[1] THEOPHILUS

Glad'st thou in such scorn?]
Theophilus, who is represented as a furious zealot for paganism, is mortified at the indifference with which Macrinus returns the happiness he had wished him by his god. Mr. M. Mason reads, Gaddest thou in such scorn? He may be right; for Macrinus is evidently anxious to pass on: the reading of the text, however, is that of all the old copies.—GIFFORD.

[2] Hand,] here used for inch, moment. We often meet the phrase of his hands, for of his inches.

[3] —flies.] This word is used by Ben Jonson, a close and devoted imitator of the ancients, for a domestic parasite, a familiar, &c. and from him, probably, Decker adopted it in the present sense.—GIFFORD.

[4] Roman angels,] i. e. the Roman eagle, the well-known military ensign. Angel in the sense of bird is frequently met with among our old writers. Jonson beautifully calls the nightingale "The dear good angel of the spring." And if this should be thought, as it probably is, a Grecism; yet we have the same term in another passage, which will admit of no dispute:

"Not an angel of the air,
Bird melodious, or bird fair," &c.
Two Noble Kinsmen.
GIFFORD.

[5] Harp. This Macrinus,
The line is, &c]
The allusion is to the rude fire-works of our ancestors. So, in the Fawne, by Marston:

"Page. There be squibs, sir, running upon lines, like some of our gawdy gallants," &c.—GIFFORD.

[6] Conster,] i. e. understand. This word (a corruption of construe), so frequently heard among the common people, has not found a place in any dictionary that I have met with.

[7] Push,] i. e. to strike a thing with such force as to dash it to pieces. The word is now obsolete; which is to be regretted, as we have none that can adequately supply its place: it is used in its proper sense by Dryden, which is the latest instance I recollect:

"Thy cunning engines have with labour raised
My heavy anger, like a mighty weight,
To fall and pash thee."
GIFFORD.

SCENE III

A Hall in Dorothea's House, with a Gallery Above.

Enter **DOROTHEA, MACRINUS,** and **ANGELO.**

DOROTHEA

My trusty Angelo, with that curious eye
Of thine, which ever waits upon my business,
I prithee watch those my still-negligent servants,
That they perform my will, in what's enjoined them
To the good of others. Be careful, my dear boy.

ANGELO
Yes, my sweetest mistress.

[Exit.

DOROTHEA
Now, sir, you may go on.

MACRINUS
I then must study
A new arithmetic, to sum up the virtues
Which Antoninus gracefully become.
There is in him so much man, so much goodness,
So much of honour, and of all things else,
Which make our being excellent, that from his store
He can enough lend others; yet, much ta'en from him,
The want shall be as little, as when seas
Lend from their bounty, to fill up the poorness
Of needy rivers.

DOROTHEA
Sir, he is more indebted
To you for praise, than you to him that owes[1] it.

MACRINUS
If queens, viewing his presents paid to the whiteness
Of your chaste hand alone, should be ambitious
But to be parted[2] in their numerous shares;
This he counts nothing: could you see main armies
Make battles in the quarrel of his valour,
That 'tis the best, the truest; this were nothing:
The greatness of his state, his father's voice,
And arm, awing Cæsarea, he ne'er boasts of;
The sunbeams which the emperor throws upon him
Shine there but as in water, and gild him
Not with one spot of pride: no, dearest beauty,
All these, heap'd up together in one scale,
Cannot weigh down the love he bears to you,
Being put into the other.

DOROTHEA
Could gold buy you

To speak thus for a friend, you, sir, are worthy
Of more than I will number; and this your language
Hath power to win upon another woman,
'Top of whose heart the feathers of this world
Are gaily stuck: but all which first you named,
And now this last, his love, to me are nothing.

MACRINUS
You make me a sad messenger;—but himself

[Enter **ANTONINUS**.

Being come in person, shall, I hope, hear from you
Music more pleasing.

ANTONINUS
Has your ear, Macrinus,
Heard none, then?

MACRINUS
None I like.

ANTONINUS
But can there be
In such a noble casket, wherein lie
Beauty and chastity in their full perfections,
A rocky heart, killing with cruelty
A life that's prostrated beneath your feet?

DOROTHEA
I am guilty of a shame I yet ne'er knew,
Thus to hold parley with you;—pray, sir, pardon.

[Going.

ANTONINUS
Good sweetness, you now have it, and shall go:
Be but so merciful, before your wounding me
With such a mortal weapon as Farewell,
To let me murmur to your virgin ear,
What I was loth to lay on any tongue
But this mine own.

DOROTHEA
If one immodest accent
Fly out, I hate you everlastingly.

ANTONINUS

My true love dares not do it.

MACRINUS
Hermes inspire thee!

[Enter, in the gallery above, **ARTEMIA, SAPRITIUS,** and **THEOPHILUS.**

ANTONINUS
Come, let me tune you:—glaze not thus your eyes
With self-love of a vow'd virginity;
All men desire your sweet society,
But if you bar me from it, you do kill me,
And of my blood are guilty.

ARTEMIA
O base villain!

SAPRITIUS
Bridle your rage, sweet princess.

ANTONINUS
Could not my fortunes,
Rear'd higher far than yours, be worthy of you,
Methinks my dear affection makes you mine.

DOROTHEA
Sir, for your fortunes, were they mines of gold,
He that I love is richer; and for worth,
You are to him lower than any slave
Is to a monarch.

SAPRITIUS
So insolent, base Christian!

DOROTHEA
Can I, with wearing out my knees before him,
Get you but be his servant, you shall boast
You're equal to a king.

SAPRITIUS
Confusion on thee,
For playing thus the lying sorceress!

ANTONINUS
Your mocks are great ones; none beneath the sun
Will I be servant to.—On my knees I beg it,
Pity me, wondrous maid.

SAPRITIUS
I curse thy baseness.

THEOPHILUS
Listen to more.

DOROTHEA
O kneel not, sir, to me.

ANTONINUS
This knee is emblem of an humbled heart:
That heart which tortured is with your disdain,
Justly for scorning others, even this heart,
To which for pity such a princess sues,
As in her hand offers me all the world,
Great Cæsar's daughter.

ARTEMIA
Slave, thou liest.

ANTONINUS
Yet this
Is adamant to her, that melts to you
In drops of blood.

THEOPHILUS
A very dog!

ANTONINUS
Perhaps
'Tis my religion makes you knit the brow;
Yet be you mine, and ever be your own:
I ne'er will screw your conscience from that Power,
On which you Christians lean.

SAPRITIUS
I can no longer
Fret out my life with weeping at thee, villain.
Sirrah! [Aloud]
Would, ere thy birth, the mighty Thunderer's hand
Had struck thee in the womb!

MACRINUS
We are betray'd.

ARTEMIA
Is that the idol, traitor, which thou kneel'st to,
Trampling upon my beauty?

THEOPHILUS
Sirrah, bandog[3]!
Wilt thou in pieces tear our Jupiter
For her? our Mars for her? our Sol for her?

ARTEMIA
Threaten not, but strike: quick vengeance flies
Into my bosom; caitiff! here all love dies.

[Exeunt above.

ANTONINUS
O! I am thunderstruck! We are both o'erwhelm'd—

MACRINUS
With one high-raging billow.

DOROTHEA
You a soldier,
And sink beneath the violence of a woman!

ANTONINUS
A woman! a wrong'd princess. From such a star
Blazing with fires of hate, what can be look'd for,
But tragical events? my life is now
The subject of her tyranny.

DOROTHEA
That fear is base,
Of death, when that death doth but life displace
Out of her house of earth; you only dread
The stroke, and not what follows when you're dead;
There's the great fear, indeed: come, let your eyes
Dwell where mine do, you'll scorn their tyrannies.

[Re-enter below, **ARTEMIA, SAPRITIUS, THEOPHILUS**, a guard; **ANGELO** comes and stands close by
DOROTHEA.

ARTEMIA
My father's nerves put vigour in mine arm,
And I his strength must use. Because I once
Shed beams of favour on thee, and, with the lion,
Play'd with thee gently, when thou struck'st my heart,
I'll not insult on a base, humbled prey,
By lingering out thy terrors; but, with one frown,
Kill thee:—hence with them all to execution.
Seize him; but let even death itself be weary

In torturing her. I'll change those smiles to shrieks;
Give the fool what she's proud of, martyrdom:
In pieces rack that pander.

[Points to **MACRINUS**.

SAPRITIUS
Albeit the reverence
I owe our gods and you, are, in my bosom,
Torrents so strong, that pity quite lies drown'd
From saving this young man; yet, when I see
What face death gives him, and that a thing within me
Says, 'tis my son, I am forced to be a man,
And grow fond of his life, which thus I beg.

ARTEMIA
And I deny.

ANTONINUS
Sir, you dishonour me,
To sue for that which I disclaim to have.
I shall more glory in my sufferings gain,
Than you in giving judgment, since I offer
My blood up to your anger; nor do I kneel
To keep a wretched life of mine from ruin:
Preserve this temple, builded fair as yours is,
And Cæsar never went in greater triumph,
Than I shall to the scaffold.

ARTEMIA
Are you so brave, sir?
Set forward to his triumph, and let those two
Go cursing along with him.

DOROTHEA
No, but pitying,
For my part, I, that you lose ten times more
By torturing me, than I that dare your tortures:
Through all the army of my sins, I have even
Labour'd to break, and cope with death to the face.
The visage of a hangman frights not me;
The sight of whips, racks, gibbets, axes, fires,
Are scaffoldings by which my soul climbs up
To an eternal habitation.

THEOPHILUS
Cæsar's imperial daughter, hear me speak.
Let not this Christian thing in this her pageantry

Of proud deriding both our gods and Cæsar,
Build to herself a kingdom in her death,
Going laughing from us: no; her bitterest torment
Shall be, to feel her constancy beaten down;
The bravery of her resolution lie
Batter'd, by argument, into such pieces,
That she again in penitence shall creep
To kiss the pavements of our paynim gods.

ARTEMIA
How to be done?

THEOPHILUS
I'll send my daughters to her,
And they shall turn her rocky faith to wax;
Else spit at me, let me be made your slave,
And meet no Roman's but a villain's grave.

ARTEMIA
Thy prisoner let her be, then; and, Sapritius,
Your son and that[4], be yours: death shall be sent
To him that suffers them, by voice or letters,
To greet each other. Rifle her estate;
Christians to beggary brought grow desperate.

DOROTHEA
Still on the bread of poverty let me feed.

ANGELO
O! my admired mistress, quench not out
The holy fires within you, though temptations
Shower down upon you: Clasp thine armour on,
Fight well, and thou shalt see, after these wars,
Thy head wear sunbeams, and thy feet touch stars.

[Exeunt.

FOOTNOTES

[1] Owes,] i. e. owns.

[2] Parted,] i. e. endowed with a part.

[3] Bandog!] A bandog, as the name imports, was a dog so fierce, as to require to be chained up. Bandogs are frequently mentioned by our old writers (indeed the word occurs three times in this play) and always with a reference to their savage nature. If the term was appropriated to a species, it probably

meant a large dog, of the mastiff kind, which, though no longer met with here, is still common in many parts of Germany: it was familiar to Snyders, and is found in most of his hunting-pieces.

In this country the bandog was kept to bait bears: with the decline of that sport, perhaps, the animal fell into disuse, as he was too ferocious for any domestic purpose. Mr. Gilchrist has furnished me with a curious passage from Laneham, which renders any further details on the subject unnecessary. "On the syxth day of her Majestyes cumming, a great sort of bandogs whear thear tyed in the utter coourt, and thyrteen bears in the inner. Whoosoever made the pannel, thear wear enoow for a queast, and one for a challenge and need wear. A wight of great wisdoom and gravitie seemed their foreman to be, had it cum to a jury: but it fell oout that they wear causd to appeer thear upon no such matter, but onlie too onswear too an auncient quarrele between them and the bandogs,"
&c. Queen Elizabeth's Entertainment at Killingwoorth Castle, in 1575.—GIFFORD.

[4] Your son and that.] Macrinus, whom before she had called a pander. M. MASON.

ACT III

SCENE I

A Room in Dorothea's House.

Enter **SAPRITIUS, THEOPHILUS, PRIEST, CALISTA**, and **CHRISTETA.**

SAPRITIUS
Sick to the death, I fear.

THEOPHILUS
I meet your sorrow,
With my true feeling of it.

SAPRITIUS
She's a witch,
A sorceress, Theophilus; my son
Is charm'd by her enchanting eyes; and, like
An image made of wax, her beams of beauty
Melt him to nothing: all my hopes in him,
And all his gotten honours, find their grave
In his strange dotage on her. Would, when first
He saw and loved her, that the earth had open'd,
And swallow'd both alive!

THEOPHILUS
There's hope left yet.

SAPRITIUS
Not any: though the princess were appeased,

All title in her love surrender'd up;
Yet this coy Christian is so transported
With her religion, that unless my son
(But let him perish first!) drink the same potion,
And be of her belief, she'll not vouchsafe
To be his lawful wife.

PRIEST
But, once removed
From her opinion, as I rest assured
The reasons of these holy maids will win her,
You'll find her tractable to any thing,
For your content or his.

THEOPHILUS
If she refuse it,
The Stygian damps, breeding infectious airs,
The mandrake's shrieks, the basilisk's killing eye,
The dreadful lightning that does crush the bones,
And never singe the skin, shall not appear
Less fatal to her, than my zeal made hot
With love unto my gods. I have deferr'd it,
In hopes to draw back this apostata,
Which will be greater honour than her death,
Unto her father's faith; and, to that end,
Have brought my daughters hither.

CALISTA
And we doubt not
To do what you desire.

SAPRITIUS
Let her be sent for.
Prosper in your good work; and were I not
To attend the princess, I would see and hear
How you succeed.

THEOPHILUS
I am commanded too,
I'll bear you company.

SAPRITIUS
Give them your ring,
To lead her as in triumph, if they win her,
Before her highness.

[Exit.

THEOPHILUS
Spare no promises,
Persuasions, or threats, I do conjure you:
If you prevail, 'tis the most glorious work
You ever undertook.

[Enter **DOROTHEA** and **ANGELO**.

PRIEST
She comes.

THEOPHILUS
We leave you;
Be constant, and be careful.

[Exeunt **THEOPHILUS** and **PRIEST**.

CALISTA
We are sorry
To meet you under guard.

DOROTHEA
But I more grieved
You are at liberty. So well I love you,
That I could wish, for such a cause as mine,
You were my fellow-prisoners: Prithee, Angelo,
Reach us some chairs. Please you sit—

CALISTA
We thank you:
Our visit is for love, love to your safety.

CHRISTETA
Our conference must be private; pray you, therefore,
Command your boy to leave us.

DOROTHEA
You may trust him
With any secret that concerns my life;
Falsehood and he are strangers: had you, ladies,
Been bless'd with such a servant, you had never
Forsook that way, your journey even half ended,
That leads to joys eternal. In the place
Of loose lascivious mirth, he would have stirr'd you
To holy meditations; and so far
He is from flattery, that he would have told you,
Your pride being at the height, how miserable
And wretched things you were, that, for an hour

Of pleasure here, have made a desperate sale
Of all your right in happiness hereafter.
He must not leave me; without him I fall:
In this life he's my servant, in the other
A wish'd companion.

ANGELO
'Tis not in the devil,
Nor all his wicked arts, to shake such goodness.

DOROTHEA
But you were speaking, lady.

CALISTA
As a friend
And lover of your safety, and I pray you
So to receive it; and, if you remember
How near in love our parents were, that we,
Even from the cradle, were brought up together,
Our amity increasing with our years,
We cannot stand suspected.

DOROTHEA
To the purpose.

CALISTA
We come, then, as good angels, Dorothea,
To make you happy; and the means so easy,
That, be not you an enemy to yourself,
Already you enjoy it.

CHRISTETA
Look on us,
Ruin'd as you are, once, and brought unto it,
By your persuasion.

CALISTA
But what follow'd, lady?
Leaving those blessings which our gods gave freely,
And shower'd upon us with a prodigal hand,
As to be noble born, youth, beauty, wealth,
And the free use of these without control,
Check, curb, or stop, such is our law's indulgence!
All happiness forsook us; bonds and fetters,
For amorous twines; the rack and hangman's whips,
In place of choice delights; our parents' curses
Instead of blessings; scorn, neglect, contempt,
Fell thick upon us.

CHRISTETA

This consider'd wisely,
We made a fair retreat; and reconciled
To our forsaken gods, we live again
In all prosperity.

CALISTA

By our example,
Bequeathing misery to such as love it,
Learn to be happy. The Christian yoke's too heavy
For such a dainty neck; it was framed rather
To be the shrine of Venus, or a pillar,
More precious than crystal, to support
Our Cupid's image: our religion, lady,
Is but a varied pleasure; yours a toil
Slaves would shrink under.

DOROTHEA

Have you not cloven feet? are you not devils?
Dare any say so much, or dare I hear it
Without a virtuous and religious anger?
Now to put on a virgin modesty,
Or maiden silence, when His power is question'd
That is omnipotent, were a greater crime,
Than in a bad cause to be impudent.
Your gods! your temples! brothel-houses rather,
Or wicked actions of the worst of men,
Pursued and practised. Your religious rites!
Oh! call them rather juggling mysteries,
The baits and nets of hell: your souls the prey
For which the devil angles; your false pleasures
A steep descent, by which you headlong fall
Into eternal torments.

CALISTA

Do not tempt
Our powerful gods.

DOROTHEA

Which of your powerful gods?
Your gold, your silver, brass, or wooden ones,
That can nor do me hurt, nor protect you?
Most pitied women! will you sacrifice
To such,—or call them gods or goddesses,
Your parents would disdain to be the same,
Or you yourselves? O blinded ignorance!
Tell me, Calista, by thy truth, I charge you,

Or any thing you hold more dear, would you,
To have him deified to posterity,
Desire your father an adulterer,
A ravisher, almost a parricide,
A vile incestuous wretch?

CALISTA
That, piety
And duty answer for me.

DOROTHEA
Or you, Christeta,
To be hereafter register'd a goddess,
Give your chaste body up to the embraces
Of wicked passion? have it writ on your forehead,
"This is the mistress in the art of sin.
Knows every trick, and labyrinth of desires
That are immodest?"

CHRISTETA
You judge better of me,
Or my affection is ill placed on you.
Shall I turn wanton?

DOROTHEA
No, I think you would not.
Yet, such was Venus, whom you worship; such
Flora, the foundress of the public stews,
And has, for that, her sacrifice; your Jupiter,
A loose adulterer:—read ye but those
That have canonized them, you'll find them worse
Than, in chaste language, I can speak them to you.
Are they immortal, then, that did partake
Of human weakness, and had ample share
In men's most base affections; subject to
Unchaste loves, anger, bondage, wounds, as men are?
Here, Jupiter, to serve his lust, turn'd bull,
The shape, indeed, in which he stole Europa;
Neptune, for gain, builds up the walls of Troy,
As a day-labourer; Apollo keeps
Admetus' sheep for bread; the Lemnian smith
Sweats at the forge for hire; Prometheus here,
With his still-growing liver, feeds the vulture;
Saturn bound fast in hell with adamant chains;
And thousands more, on whom abused error
Bestows a deity. Will you then, dear sisters,
For I would have you such, pay your devotions
To things of less power than yourselves?

CALISTA
We worship
Their good deeds in their images.

DOROTHEA
By whom fashion'd?
By sinful men. I'll tell you a short tale[1],
Nor can you but confess it is a true one:
A king of Egypt, being to erect
The image of Osiris, whom they honour,
Took from the matrons' necks the richest jewels,
And purest gold, as the materials
To finish up his work; which perfected,
With all solemnity he set it up,
To be adored, and served himself his idol;
Desiring it to give him victory
Against his enemies: but, being overthrown,
Enraged against his god, (these are fine gods,
Subject to human fury!) he took down
The senseless thing, and melting it again,
He made a bason, in which eunuchs wash'd
His concubine's feet; and for this sordid use,
Some months it served: his mistress proving false,
As most indeed do so, and grace concluded
Between him and the priests, of the same bason
He made his god again!—Think, think, of this,
And then consider, if all worldly honours,
Or pleasures that do leave sharp stings behind them,
Have power to win such as have reasonable souls,
To put their trust in dross.

CALISTA
Oh, that I had been born
Without a father!

CHRISTETA
Piety to him
Hath ruin'd us for ever.

DOROTHEA
Think not so;
You may repair all yet: the attribute
That speaks his Godhead most, is merciful:
Revenge is proper to the fiends you worship,
Yet cannot strike without his leave.—You weep,—
Oh, 'tis a heavenly shower! celestial balm
To cure your wounded conscience! let it fall,

Fall thick upon it; and, when that is spent,
I'll help it with another of my tears:
And may your true repentance prove the child
Of my true sorrow, never mother had
A birth so happy!

CALISTA
We are caught ourselves,
That came to take you; and, assured of conquest,
We are your captives.

DOROTHEA
And in that you triumph:
Your victory had been eternal loss,
And this your loss immortal gain. Fix here,
And you shall feel yourselves inwardly arm'd
'Gainst tortures, death, and hell:—but, take heed, sisters,
That, or through weakness, threats, or mild persuasions,
Though of a father, you fall not into
A second and a worse apostasy.

CALISTA
Never, oh never! steel'd by your example,
We dare the worst of tyranny.

CHRISTETA
Here's our warrant,
You shall along and witness it.

DOROTHEA
Be confirm'd then;
And rest assured, the more you suffer here,
The more your glory, you to heaven more dear.

[Exeunt.

FOOTNOTE

[1] —I'll tell you a short tale, &c.] I once thought that I had read this short tale in Arnobius, from whom, and from Augustin, much of the preceding speech is taken; but, upon looking him over again, I can scarcely find a trace of it. Herodotus has, indeed, a story of a king of Egypt (Amasis), which bears a distant resemblance to it; but the application is altogether different:—there is a bason of gold in which he and his guests were accustomed to spit, wash their feet, &c. which is formed into a god; but whether this furnished the poet with any hints I cannot undertake to say.—GIFFORD.

The Governor's Palace.

Enter **ARTEMIA, SAPRITIUS, THEOPHILUS**, and **HARPAX**.

ARTEMIA
Sapritius, though your son deserve no pity,
We grieve his sickness: his contempt of us
We cast behind us, and look back upon
His service done to Cæsar, that weighs down
Our just displeasure. If his malady
Have growth from his restraint, or that you think
His liberty can cure him, let him have it:
Say, we forgive him freely.

SAPRITIUS
Your grace binds us
Ever your humblest vassals.

ARTEMIA
Use all means
For his recovery; though yet I love him,
I will not force affection. If the Christian,
Whose beauty hath out-rivall'd me, be won
To be of our belief, then let him wed her;
That all may know, when the cause wills, I can
Command my own affections.

THEOPHILUS
Be happy then,
My lord Sapritius: I am confident,
Such eloquence and sweet persuasion dwell
Upon my daughters' tongues, that they will work her
To any thing they please.

SAPRITIUS
I wish they may!
Yet 'tis no easy task to undertake,
To alter a perverse and obstinate woman.

[A shout within: loud music.

ARTEMIA
What means this shout?

SAPRITIUS
It is seconded with music,

Triumphant music.—Ha!

[Enter **SEMPRONIUS**.

SEMPRONIUS
My lord, your daughters,
The pillars of our faith[1], having converted,
For so report gives out, the Christian lady,
The image of great Jupiter born before them,
Sue for access.

THEOPHILUS
My soul divined as much.
Blest be the time when first they saw this light!
Their mother, when she bore them to support
My feeble age, fill'd not my longing heart
With so much joy, as they in this good work
Have thrown upon me.

[Enter **PRIEST** with the Image of Jupiter, incense and censers: followed by **CALISTA** and **CHRISTETA**, leading **DOROTHEA**.

Welcome, oh, thrice welcome,
Daughters, both of my body and my mind!
Let me embrace in you my bliss, my comfort;
And, Dorothea, now more welcome too,
Than if you never had fallen off! I am ravish'd
With the excess of joy:—speak, happy daughters,
The blest event.

CALISTA
We never gain'd so much
By any undertaking.

THEOPHILUS
O my dear girl,
Our gods reward thee!

DOROTHEA
Nor was ever time,
On my part, better spent.

CHRISTETA
We are all now
Of one opinion.

THEOPHILUS
My best Christeta!

Madam, if ever you did grace to worth,
Vouchsafe your princely hands.

ARTEMIA
Most willingly—
Do you refuse it?

CALISTA
Let us first deserve it.

THEOPHILUS
My own child still! here set our god; prepare
The incense quickly: Come, fair Dorothea,
I will myself support you;—now kneel down,
And pay your vows to Jupiter.

DOROTHEA
I shall do it
Better by their example.

THEOPHILUS
They shall guide you;
They are familiar with the sacrifice.
Forward, my twins of comfort, and, to teach her,
Make a joint offering.

CHRISTETA
Thus—

[They both spit at the image.

CALISTA
And thus—

[Throw it down, and spurn it.

HARPAX
Profane,
And impious! stand you now like a statue?
Are you the champion of the gods? where is
Your holy zeal, your anger?

THEOPHILUS
I am blasted;
And, as my feet were rooted here, I find
I have no motion; I would I had no sight too!
Or if my eyes can serve to any use,
Give me, thou injured power! a sea of tears,

To expiate this madness in my daughters;
For, being themselves, they would have trembled at
So blasphemous a deed in any other:—
For my sake, hold awhile thy dreadful thunder,
And give me patience to demand a reason
For this accursed act.

DOROTHEA
'Twas bravely done.

THEOPHILUS
Peace, damn'd enchantress, peace!—I should look on you
With eyes made red with fury, and my hand,
That shakes with rage, should much outstrip my tongue,
And seal my vengeance on your hearts;—but nature,
To you that have fallen once, bids me again
To be a father. Oh! how durst you tempt
The anger of great Jove?

DOROTHEA
Alack, poor Jove!
He is no swaggerer; how still he stands!
He'll take a kick, or any thing.

SAPRITIUS
Stop her mouth.

DOROTHEA
It is the patient'st godling! do not fear him;
He would not hurt the thief that stole away
Two of his golden locks; indeed he could not:
And still 'tis the same quiet thing.

THEOPHILUS
Blasphemer!
Ingenious cruelty shall punish this:
Thou art past hope: but for you yet, dear daughters,
Again bewitch'd, the dew of mild forgiveness
May gently fall, provided you deserve it,
With true contrition: be yourselves again;
Sue to the offended deity.

CHRISTETA
Not to be
The mistress of the earth.

CALISTA
I will not offer

A grain of incense to it, much less kneel,
Nor look on it but with contempt and scorn,
To have a thousand years conferr'd upon me
Of worldly blessings. We profess ourselves
To be, like Dorothea, Christians;
And owe her for that happiness.

THEOPHILUS
My ears
Receive, in hearing this, all deadly charms,
Powerful to make man wretched.

ARTEMIA
Are these they
You bragg'd could convert others!

SAPRITIUS
That want strength
To stand themselves!

HARPAX
Your honour is engaged,
The credit of your cause depends upon it;
Something you must do suddenly.

THEOPHILUS
And I will.

HARPAX
They merit death; but, falling by your hand,
'Twill be recorded for a just revenge,
And holy fury in you.

THEOPHILUS
Do not blow
The furnace of a wrath thrice hot already;
Ætna is in my breast, wildfire burns here,
Which only blood must quench. Incensed Power!
Which from my infancy I have adored,
Look down with favourable beams upon
The sacrifice, though not allow'd thy priest,
Which I will offer to thee; and be pleased,
My fiery zeal inciting me to act,
To call that justice others may style murder.
Come, you accursed, thus by the hair I drag you
Before this holy altar; thus look on you,
Less pitiful than tigers to their prey:
And thus, with mine own hand, I take that life

Which I gave to you.

[Kills them.

DOROTHEA
O most cruel butcher!

THEOPHILUS
My anger ends not here: hell's dreadful porter,
Receive into thy ever-open gates
Their damned souls, and let the Furies' whips
On them alone be wasted; and, when death
Closes these eyes, 'twill be Elysium to me
To hear their shrieks and howlings. Make me, Pluto,
Thy instrument to furnish thee with souls
Of that accursed sect; nor let me fall,
Till my fell vengeance hath consumed them all.

[Exit, with **HARPAX**.

ARTEMIA
'Tis a brave zeal.

[Enter **ANGELO**, smiling.

DOROTHEA
Oh, call him back again,
Call back your hangman! here's one prisoner left
To be the subject of his knife.

ARTEMIA
Not so;
We are not so near reconciled unto thee;
Thou shalt not perish such an easy way.
Be she your charge, Sapritius, now; and suffer
None to come near her, till we have found out
Some torments worthy of her.

ANGELO
Courage, mistress;
These martyrs but prepare your glorious fate:
You shall exceed them, and not imitate.

[Exeunt.

FOOTNOTE

[1] The pillars of our faith, &c.] Here, as in many other places, the language of Christianity and paganism is confounded: faith was always the distinctive term for the former, in opposition to heathenism. —GIFFORD.

ACT IV

SCENE I

The Governor's Palace.

ANTONINUS on a couch, asleep, with **DOCTORS** about him; **SAPRITIUS** and **MACRINUS**.

SAPRITIUS
O you, that are half gods, lengthen that life
Their deities lend us; turn o'er all the volumes
Of your mysterious Æsculapian science,
T' increase the number of this young man's days:
And, for each minute of his time prolong'd,
Your fee shall be a piece of Roman gold
With Cæsar's stamp, such as he sends his captains
When in the wars they earn well: do but save him,
And, as he's half myself, be you all mine.

1ˢᵗ DOCTOR
What art can do, we promise; physic's hand
As apt is to destroy as to preserve,
If heaven make not the med'cine: all this while,
Our skill hath combat held with his disease;
But 'tis so arm'd, and a deep melancholy,
To be such in part with death, we are in fear
The grave must mock our labours.

MACRINUS
I have been
His keeper in this sickness, with such eyes
As I have seen my mother watch o'er me.
Stand by his pillow, and, in his broken slumbers,
Him shall you hear cry out on Dorothea;
And, when his arms fly open to catch her,
Closing together, he falls fast asleep,
Pleased with embracings of her airy form.
Physicians but torment him; his disease
Laughs at their gibberish language: let him hear
The voice of Dorothea, nay, but the name,
He starts up with high colour in his face:
She, or none, cures him; and how that can be,

The princess' strict command barring that happiness,
To me impossible seems.

SAPRITIUS
To me it shall not;
I'll be no subject to the greatest Cæsar
Was ever crown'd with laurel, rather than cease
To be a father.

[Exit.

MACRINUS
Silence, sir; he wakes.

ANTONINUS
Thou kill'st me, Dorothea; oh, Dorothea!

MACRINUS
She's here

ANTONINUS
Here! Where? Why do you mock me, sir?
Age on my head hath stuck no white hairs yet,
Yet I'm an old man, a fond doting fool
Upon a woman. I, to buy her beauty,
(In truth I am bewitch'd) offer my life,
And she, for my acquaintance, hazards hers:
Yet, for our equal sufferings, none holds out
A hand of pity.

1ˢᵗ DOCTOR
Let him have some music.

ANTONINUS
Hell on your fiddling!

[Starting from his couch.

1ˢᵗ DOCTOR
Take again your bed, sir;
Sleep is a sovereign physic.

ANTONINUS
Confusion on your fooleries! Where's the rest
Thy pills and base apothecary drugs
Threaten'd to bring unto me? Out, you impostors!
Quacksalving, cheating mountebanks! your skill
Is to make sound men sick, and sick men kill.

MACRINUS
Oh, be yourself, dear friend.

ANTONINUS
Myself, Macrinus!
How can I be myself, when I am mangled
Into a thousand pieces? here moves my head,
But where's my heart? wherever—that lies dead.

[Re-enter **SAPRITIUS**, dragging in **DOROTHEA** by the hair, **ANGELO** following.

SAPRITIUS
Follow me, thou damn'd sorceress! Call up thy spirits,
And, if they can, now let them from my hand
Untwine these witching hairs.

ANTONINUS
I am that spirit:
Or, if I be not, were you not my father,
One made of iron should hew that hand in pieces,
That so defaces this sweet monument
Of my love's beauty.

SAPRITIUS
Art thou sick?

ANTONINUS
To death.

SAPRITIUS
Would'st thou recover?

ANTONINUS
Would I live in bliss!

SAPRITIUS
And do thine eyes shoot daggers at that man
That brings thee health?

ANTONINUS
It is not in the world.

SAPRITIUS
It's here.

ANTONINUS
To treasure, by enchantment lock'd

In caves as deep as hell, am I as near.

1st DOCTOR
Shall the boy stay, sir?

SAPRITIUS
No matter for the boy.

[Exeunt **SAPRITIUS, MACRINUS** and **DOCTOR**.

DOROTHEA
O, guard me, angels!
What tragedy must begin now?

ANTONINUS
When a tiger
Leaps into a timorous herd, with ravenous jaws,
Being hunger-starved, what tragedy then begins?

DOROTHEA
Death; I am happy so: you, hitherto,
Have still had goodness sphered within your eyes;
Let not that orb be broken.

ANGELO
Fear not, mistress;
If he dare offer violence, we two
Are strong enough for such a sickly man.

DOROTHEA
What is your horrid purpose, sir? your eye
Bears danger in it.

ANTONINUS
I must—

DOROTHEA
Oh, kill me,

[Kneels.

And heaven will take it as a sacrifice;
But, if you play the ravisher, there is
A hell to swallow you.

ANTONINUS
Rise:—for the Roman empire, Dorothea,
I would not wound thine honour. My father's will

Would have me seize upon you, as my prey;
Which I abhor, as much as the blackest sin
The villany of man did ever act.

[**SAPRITIUS** breaks in with **MACRINUS**.

DOROTHEA
Die happy for this language!

SAPRITIUS
Die a slave,
A blockish idiot!

MACRINUS
Dear sir, vex him not.

SAPRITIUS
Yes, and vex thee too: where's this lamia[1]?

DOROTHEA
I'm here; do what you please.

SAPRITIUS
Spurn her to the bar.

DOROTHEA
Come, boy, being there, more near to heaven we are.

SAPRITIUS
Kick harder; go out, witch!

[Exeunt.

ANTONINUS
O bloody hangmen! Thine own gods give thee breath!
Each of thy tortures is my several death.

[Exit.

FOOTNOTE

[1] Lamia,] i. e. sorceress, hag. The word is pure Latin.

SCENE II [1]

The Place of Execution. A scaffold, Block, &c.

Enter **ANTONINUS**, supported by **MACRINUS**, and **SERVANTS**.

ANTONINUS
Is this the place, where virtue is to suffer,
And heavenly beauty, leaving this base earth,
To make a glad return from whence it came?
Is it, Macrinus?

MACRINUS
By this preparation,
You well may rest assured that Dorothea
This hour is to die here.

ANTONINUS
Then with her dies
The abstract of all sweetness that's in woman!
Set me down, friend, that, ere the iron hand
Of death close up mine eyes, they may at once
Take my last leave both of this light and her:
For, she being gone, the glorious sun himself
To me's Cimmerian darkness.

MACRINUS
Strange affection[2]!
Cupid once more hath changed his shafts with Death,
And kills, instead of giving life.

ANTONINUS
Nay, weep not;
Though tears of friendship be a sovereign balm,
On me they're cast away. It is decreed
That I must die with her; our clue of life
Was spun together.

MACRINUS
Yet, sir, 'tis my wonder,
That you, who, hearing only what she suffers,
Partake of all her tortures, yet will be,
To add to your calamity, an eyewitness
Of her last tragic scene, which must pierce deeper,
And make the wound more desperate.

ANTONINUS
Oh, Macrinus!
'Twould linger out my torments else, not kill me,
Which is the end I aim at: being to die too,

What instrument more glorious can I wish for,
Than what is made sharp by my constant love
And true affection? It may be, the duty
And loyal service, with which I pursued her,
And seal'd it with my death, will be remember'd
Among her blessed actions; and what honour
Can I desire beyond it?

[Enter a **GUARD** bringing in **DOROTHEA**, a **HEADSMAN** before her; followed by **THEOPHILUS**, **SAPRITIUS**, and **HARPAX**.

See, she comes;
How sweet her innocence appears! more like
To heaven itself, than any sacrifice
That can be offer'd to it. By my hopes
Of joys hereafter, the sight makes me doubtful
In my belief; nor can I think our gods
Are good, or to be served, that take delight
In offerings of this kind: that, to maintain
Their power, deface the master-piece of nature,
Which they themselves come short of. She ascends,
And every step raises her nearer heaven.

SAPRITIUS
You are to blame
To let him come abroad.

MACRINUS
It was his will;
And we were left to serve him, not command him.

ANTONINUS
Good sir, be not offended; nor deny
My last of pleasures in this happy object,
That I shall e'er be blest with.

THEOPHILUS
Now, proud contemner
Of us, and of our gods, tremble to think,
It is not in the Power thou serv'st to save thee.
Not all the riches of the sea, increased
By violent shipwrecks, nor the unsearch'd mines,
(Mammon's unknown exchequer), shall redeem thee:
And, therefore, having first with horror weigh'd
What 'tis to die, and to die young; to part with
All pleasures and delights; lastly, to go
Where all antipathies to comfort dwell,
Furies behind, about thee, and before thee;

And, to add to affliction, the remembrance
Of the Elysian joys thou might'st have tasted,
Hadst thou not turn'd apostata[3] to those gods
That so reward their servants; let despair
Prevent the hangman's sword, and on this scaffold
Make thy first entrance into hell.

ANTONINUS
She smiles,
Unmoved, by Mars! as if she were assured
Death, looking on her constancy, would forget
The use of his inevitable hand.

THEOPHILUS
Derided too! despatch, I say.

DOROTHEA
Thou fool!
That gloriest in having power to ravish
A trifle from me I am weary of,
What is this life to me? not worth a thought;
Or, if it be esteem'd, 'tis that I lose it
To win a better: even thy malice serves
To me but as a ladder to mount up
To such a height of happiness, where I shall
Look down with scorn on thee, and on the world;
Where, circled with true pleasures, placed above
The reach of death or time, 'twill be my glory
To think at what an easy price I bought it.
There's a perpetual spring, perpetual youth:
No joint-benumbing cold, or scorching heat,
Famine, nor age, have any being there.
Forget, for shame, your Tempe; bury in
Oblivion your feign'd Hesperian orchards:—
The golden fruit, kept by the watchful dragon,
Which did require a Hercules to get[4] it,
Compared with what grows in all plenty there,
Deserves not to be named. The Power I serve
Laughs at your happy Araby, or the
Elysian shades; for he hath made his bowers
Better in deed, than you can fancy yours.

ANTONINUS
O, take me thither with you!

DOROTHEA
Trace my steps, And be assured you shall.

SAPRITIUS

With my own hands
I'll rather stop that little breath is left thee,
And rob thy killing fever.

THEOPHILUS

By no means;
Let him go with her: do, seduced young man,
And wait upon thy saint in death; do, do:
And, when you come to that imagined place,
That place of all delights—pray you, observe me,
And meet those cursed things I once call'd Daughters,
Whom I have sent as harbingers before you;
If there be any truth in your religion,
In thankfulness to me, that with care hasten
Your journey thither, pray you send me some
Small pittance of that curious fruit you boast of.

ANTONINUS

Grant that I may go with her, and I will.

SAPRITIUS

Wilt thou in thy last minute damn thyself?

THEOPHILUS

The gates to hell are open.

DOROTHEA

Know, thou tyrant,
Thou agent for the devil, thy great master,
Though thou art most unworthy to taste of it,
I can, and will.

[Enter **ANGELO**, in the Angel's habit[5].

HARPAX

Oh! mountains fall upon me,
Or hide me in the bottom of the deep,
Where light may never find me!

THEOPHILUS

What's the matter?

SAPRITIUS

This is prodigious, and confirms her witchcraft.

THEOPHILUS

Harpax, my Harpax, speak!

HARPAX
I dare not stay:
Should I but hear her once more, I were lost.
Some whirlwind snatch me from this cursed place,
To which compared, (and with what now I suffer,)
Hell's torments are sweet slumbers!

[Exit.

SAPRITIUS
Follow him.

THEOPHILUS
He is distracted, and I must not lose him.
Thy charms upon my servant, cursed witch,
Give thee a short reprieve. Let her not die,
Till my return.

[Exeunt **SAPRITIUS** and **THEOPHILUS**.

ANTONINUS
She minds him not; what object
Is her eye fix'd on?

MACRINUS
I see nothing.

ANTONINUS
Mark her.

DOROTHEA
Thou glorious minister of the Power I serve!
(For thou art more than mortal,) is 't for me,
Poor sinner, thou art pleased awhile to leave
Thy heavenly habitation, and vouchsafest,
Though glorified, to take my servant's habit?—
For, put off thy divinity, so look'd
My lovely Angelo.

ANGELO
Know, I am the same;
And still the servant to your piety.
Your zealous prayers and pious deeds first won me
(But 'twas by His command to whom you sent them)
To guide your steps. I tried your charity,
When in a beggar's shape you took me up,
And clothed my naked limbs, and after fed,

As you believed, my famish'd mouth. Learn all,
By your example, to look on the poor
With gentle eyes! for in such habits, often,
Angels desire an alms[6]. I never left you,
Nor will I now; for I am sent to carry
Your pure and innocent soul to joys eternal,
Your martyrdom once suffer'd; and before it,
Ask any thing from me, and rest assured,
You shall obtain it.

DOROTHEA
I am largely paid
For all my torments. Since I find such grace,
Grant that the love of this young man to me,
In which he languisheth to death, may be
Changed to the love of heaven.

ANGELO
I will perform it;
And in that instant when the sword sets free
Your happy soul, his shall have liberty.
Is there aught else?

DOROTHEA
For proof that I forgive
My persecutor, who in scorn desired
To taste of that most sacred fruit I go to;
After my death, as sent from me, be pleased
To give him of it.

ANGELO
Willingly, dear mistress.

MACRINUS
I am amazed.

ANTONINUS
I feel a holy fire,
That yields a comfortable heat within me;
I am quite alter'd from the thing I was.
See! I can stand, and go alone; thus kneel
To heavenly Dorothea, touch her hand
With a religious kiss.

[Kneels.

[Re-enter **SAPRITIUS** and **THEOPHILUS**.

SAPRITIUS
He is well now,
But will not be drawn back.

THEOPHILUS
It matters not,
We can discharge this work without his help.
But see your son.

SAPRITIUS
Villain!

ANTONINUS
Sir, I beseech you,
Being so near our ends, divorce us not.

THEOPHILUS
I'll quickly make a separation of them:
Hast thou aught else to say?

DOROTHEA
Nothing, but to blame
Thy tardiness in sending me to rest;
My peace is made with heaven, to which my soul
Begins to take her flight: strike, O! strike quickly;
And, though you are unmoved to see my death,
Hereafter, when my story shall be read,
As they were present now, the hearers shall
Say this of Dorothea, with wet eyes,
"She lived a virgin, and a virgin dies."

[Her head is struck off.

ANTONINUS
O, take my soul along, to wait on thine!

MACRINUS
Your son sinks too.

[**ANTONINUS** falls.

SAPRITIUS
Already dead!

THEOPHILUS
Die all
That are, or favour this accursed sect:
I triumph in their ends, and will raise up

A hill of their dead carcasses, to o'erlook
The Pyrenean hills, but I'll root out
These superstitious fools, and leave the world
No name of Christian.

[Loud music: Exit **ANGELO**, having first laid his hand upon the mouths of **ANTONINUS** and **DOROTHEA**.

SAPRITIUS
Ha! heavenly music!

MACRINUS
'Tis in the air.

THEOPHILUS
Illusions of the devil,
Wrought by some witch of her religion,
That fain would make her death a miracle;
It frights not me. Because he is your son,
Let him have burial; but let her body
Be cast forth with contempt in some highway,
And be to vultures and to dogs a prey.

[Exeunt.

[**THEOPHILUS** discovered sitting in his Study: books about him[7].

THEOPHILUS
Is 't holiday, O Cæsar, that thy servant,
Thy provost, to see execution done
On these base Christians in Cæsarea,
Should now want work? Sleep these idolaters,
That none are stirring?—As a curious painter,
When he has made some honourable piece,
Stands off, and with a searching eye examines
Each colour, how 'tis sweeten'd; and then hugs
Himself for his rare workmanship—so here,
Will I my drolleries, and bloody landscapes,
Long past wrapt up, unfold, to make me merry
With shadows, now I want the substances.
My muster-book of hell-hounds. Were the Christians,
Whose names stand here, alive and arm'd, not Rome
Could move upon her hinges. What I've done,
Or shall hereafter, is not out of hate
To poor tormented wretches[8]; no, I'm carried
With violence of zeal, and streams of service
I owe our Roman gods. This Christian maid was well,

[Enter **ANGELO** with a basket filled with fruit and flowers.

A pretty one; but let such horror follow
The next I feed with torments, that when Rome
Shall hear it, her foundation at the sound
May feel an earthquake. How now?

[Music.

ANGELO
Are you amazed, sir?
So great a Roman spirit—and doth it tremble!

THEOPHILUS
How cam'st thou in? to whom thy business?

ANGELO
To you:
I had a mistress, late sent hence by you
Upon a bloody errand; you entreated,
That, when she came into that blessed garden
Whither she knew she went, and where, now happy,
She feeds upon all joy, she would send to you
Some of that garden fruit and flowers; which here,
To have her promise saved, are brought by me.

THEOPHILUS
Cannot I see this garden?

ANGELO
Yes, if the master
Will give you entrance.

[He vanishes.

THEOPHILUS
'Tis a tempting fruit,
And the most bright-cheek'd child I ever view'd;
Sweet smelling, goodly fruit. What flowers are these?
In Dioclesian's gardens, the most beauteous,
Compared with these, are weeds: is it not February,
The second day she died? frost, ice, and snow,
Hang on the beard of winter: where's the sun
That gilds this summer? pretty, sweet boy, say,
In what country shall a man find this garden?—
My delicate boy,—gone! vanish'd! within there,
Julianus! Geta!—

[Enter **JULIANUS** and **GETA**.

BOTH
My lord.

THEOPHILUS
Are my gates shut?

GETA
And guarded.

THEOPHILUS
Saw you not
A boy?

JULIANUS
Where?

THEOPHILUS
Here he enter'd; a young lad;
A thousand blessings danced upon his eyes:
A smoothfaced, glorious thing, that brought this basket.

GETA
No, sir!

THEOPHILUS
Away—but be in reach, if my voice calls you.

[Exeunt **JULIANUS** and **GETA**.

No!—vanish'd, and not seen!—Be thou a spirit,
Sent from that witch to mock me, I am sure
This is essential, and, howe'er it grows,
Will taste it.

[Eats of the fruit.

HARPAX [within.]
Ha, ha, ha, ha!

THEOPHILUS
So good I'll have some more, sure.

HARPAX
Ha, ha, ha, ha! great liquorish fool!

THEOPHILUS
What art thou?

HARPAX
A fisherman.

THEOPHILUS
What dost thou catch?

HARPAX
Souls, souls; a fish call'd souls.

THEOPHILUS
Geta!

[Re-enter **GETA**.

GETA
My lord.

HARPAX [within.]
Ha, ha, ha, ha!

THEOPHILUS
What insolent slave is this, dares laugh at me?
Or what is 't the dog grins at so?

GETA
I neither know, my lord, at what, nor
whom; for there is none without, but my fellow
Julianus, and he is making a garland for Jupiter.

THEOPHILUS
Jupiter! all within me is not well;
And yet not sick.

HARPAX [within.]
Ha, ha, ha, ha!

THEOPHILUS
What's thy name, slave?

HARPAX [At one end of the room.]
Go look.

GETA
'Tis Harpax' voice.

THEOPHILUS
Harpax! go, drag the caitiff to my foot,

That I may stamp upon him.

HARPAX [at the other end.]
Fool, thou liest!

GETA
He's yonder, now, my lord.

THEOPHILUS
Watch thou that end,
Whilst I make good this.

HARPAX [in the middle.]
Ha, ha, ha, ha, ha!

THEOPHILUS
Search for him.

[Exit **GETA**.]

All this ground, methinks, is bloody,
And paved with thousands of those Christians' eyes
Whom I have tortured; and they stare upon me.
What was this apparition? sure it had
A shape angelical. Mine eyes, though dazzled,
And daunted at first sight, tell me, it wore
A pair of glorious wings; yes, they were wings;
And hence he flew:—'tis vanish'd! Jupiter,
For all my sacrifices done to him,
Never once gave me smile.—How can stone smile?
Or wooden image laugh?

[Music.]

Ha! I remember,
Such music gave a welcome to mine ear,
When the fair youth came to me:—'tis in the air,
Or from some better place; a Power divine,
Through my dark ignorance, on my soul does shine,
And makes me see a conscience all stain'd o'er,
Nay, drown'd and damn'd for ever in Christian gore.

HARPAX [within.]
Ha, ha, ha!

THEOPHILUS
Again!—What dainty relish on my tongue
This fruit hath left! some angel hath me fed:

If so toothful, I will be banqueted.

[Eats again.

[Enter **HARPAX**, in a fearful shape, fire flashing out of the Study.

HARPAX
Hold!

THEOPHILUS
Not for Cæsar.

HARPAX
But for me thou shalt.

THEOPHILUS
Thou art no twin to him that last was here.
Ye Powers, whom my soul bids me reverence, guard me!
What art thou?

HARPAX
I am thy master.

THEOPHILUS
Mine!

HARPAX
And thou my everlasting slave: that Harpax,
Who hand in hand hath led thee to thy hell,
Am I.

THEOPHILUS
Avaunt!

HARPAX
I will not; cast thou down
That basket with the things in 't, and fetch up
What thou hast swallow'd, and then take a drink,
Which I shall give thee, and I'm gone.

THEOPHILUS
My fruit!
Does this offend thee? see!

[Eats again.

HARPAX
Spit it to the earth,

And tread upon it, or I'll piecemeal tear thee.

THEOPHILUS
Art thou with this affrighted? see, here's more.

[Pulls out a handful of flowers.

HARPAX
Fling them away, I'll take thee else, and hang thee
In a contorted chain of icicles,
In the frigid zone: down with them!

THEOPHILUS
At the bottom
One thing I found not yet. See!

[Holds up a cross of flowers.

HARPAX
Oh! I am tortured.

THEOPHILUS
Can this do 't? hence, thou fiend infernal, hence!

HARPAX
Clasp Jupiter's image, and away with that.

THEOPHILUS
At thee I'll fling that Jupiter; for, methinks,
I serve a better master: he now checks me
For murdering my two daughters, put on[9] by thee.
By thy damn'd rhetoric did I hunt the life
Of Dorothea, the holy virgin-martyr.
She is not angry with the axe, nor me,
But sends these presents to me; and I'll travel
O'er worlds to find her, and from her white hand
Beg a forgiveness.

HARPAX
No; I'll bind thee here.

THEOPHILUS
I serve a strength above thine; this small weapon[10],
Methinks, is armour hard enough.

HARPAX
Keep from me.

[Sinks a little.

THEOPHILUS
Art posting to thy centre? down, hell-hound! down!
Me thou hast lost. That arm, which hurls thee hence,

[**HARPAX** disappears.

Save me, and set me up, the strong defence
In the fair Christian quarrel!

[Enter **ANGELO**.

ANGELO
Fix thy foot there,
Nor be thou shaken with a Cæsar's voice,
Though thousand deaths were in it; and I then
Will bring thee to a river, that shall wash
Thy bloody hands clean and more white than snow;
And to that garden where these blest things grow,
And to that martyr'd virgin, who hath sent
That heavenly token to thee: spread this brave wing,
And serve, than Cæsar, a far greater king.

[Exit.

THEOPHILUS
It is, it is, some angel. Vanish'd again!
Oh, come back, ravishing boy! bright messenger!
Thou hast, by these mine eyes fix'd on thy beauty,
Illumined all my soul. Now look I back
On my black tyrannies, which, as they did
Outdare the bloodiest, thou, blest spirit, that lead'st me,
Teach me what I must do, and, to do well,
That my last act the best may parallel[11].

[Exit.

FOOTNOTES

[1] *Speaking of the remainder of this act, Gifford says, "there may be (and probably are) finer passages in our dramatic poets, but I am not acquainted with them."*

[2] *Mac. Strange affection!*
Cupid once more hath changed his shafts with Death,
And kills, instead of giving life.]

This is a beautiful allusion to a little poem among the Elegies of Secundus. Cupid and Death unite in the destruction of a lover, and in endeavouring to recover their weapons from the body of the victim, commit a mutual mistake, each plucking out the "shafts" of the other. The consequences of this are prettily described:

Missa peregrinis sparguntur vulnera nervis,
Et manus ignoto sævit utrinque malo.
Irrita Mors arcus validi molimina damnat,
Plorat Amor teneras tam valuisse manus;
Foedabant juvenes primus in pulvere malas
Oscula quas, heu, ad blanda vocabat Amor.
Canicies vernis florebat multa corollis
Persephone crinem vulserat unde sibi.
Quid facerent? falsas procul abjecere sagittas,
De pharetra jaculum prompsit uterque novum.
Res bona! sed virus pueri penetravit in arcum;
Ex illo miseros tot dedit ille neci. Lib. ii. Eleg. 6.

The fable, however, is very ancient.—GIFFORD.

[3] Apostata.] Our old writers usually said, apostata, statua, &c. where we now say, apostate, statue.

[4] Which did require a Hercules to get it.] This beautiful description of Elysium, as Mr. Gilchrist observes to me, has been imitated by Nabbes, in that very poetic rhapsody, Microcosmus: some of the lines may be given:

"Cold there compels no use of rugged furs,
Nor makes the mountains barren; there's no dog
To rage, and scorch the land. Spring's always there,
And paints the valleys; whilst a temperate air
Sweeps their embroider'd face with his curl'd gales,
And breathes perfumes:—there night doth never spread
Her ebon wings: but daylight's always there,
And one blest season crowns the eternal year."
GIFFORD.

[5] Enter ANGELO, in the Angel's habit, &c.] It appears that Angelo was not meant to be seen or heard by any of the people present, but Dorothea. In the inventory of the Lord Admiral's properties, given by Mr. Malone, is, "a roobe for to goe invisibell." It was probably of a light gauzy texture, and afforded a sufficient hint to our ancestors, not to see the person invested with it; or rather, to understand that some of the characters on the stage were not to see him.—GIFFORD.

[6] —Learn all,
By your example, &c.]
"Be not forgetful to entertain strangers; for thereby some have entertained angels unawares." Heb. c. xiii. v. 2. Here is also a beautiful allusion to the parting speech of the "sociable archangel," to Tobit and his son.—GIFFORD.

[7] The whole of this scene Gifford ascribes to Decker.

[8] —is not out of hate
To poor tormented wretches, &c.]
This is said to distinguish his character from that of Sapritius, whose zeal is influenced by motives of interest, and by many other considerations, which appear to weigh nothing with Theophilus.—GIFFORD.

[9] Put on,] i. e. instigated.

[10] —this small weapon.] Meaning the "cross of flowers," which he had just found. The language and ideas of this play are purely catholic.—GIFFORD.

[11] That my last act the best may parallel.] Thus far Decker; what follows, I apprehend, was written by Massinger. In pathos, strength, and harmony, it is not surpassed by any passage of equal length in the English language.—GIFFORD.

SCENE II

Dioclesian's Palace

Enter **DIOCLESIAN, MAXIMINUS**, the **KINGS** of Epire, Pontus, and Macedon, meeting **ARTEMIA**; **ATTENDANTS**.

ARTEMIA
Glory and conquest still attend upon
Triumphant Cæsar!

DIOCLESIAN
Let thy wish, fair daughter,
Be equally divided; and hereafter
Learn thou to know and reverence Maximinus,
Whose power, with mine united, makes one Cæsar.

MAXIMINUS
But that I fear 'twould be held flattery,
The bonds consider'd in which we stand tied,
As love and empire, I should say, till now
I ne'er had seen a lady I thought worthy
To be my mistress.

ARTEMIA
Sir, you show yourself
Both courtier and soldier; but take heed,
Take heed, my lord, though my dull-pointed beauty,
Stain'd by a harsh refusal in my servant,
Cannot dart forth such beams as may inflame you,

You may encounter such a powerful one,
That with a pleasing heat will thaw your heart,
Though bound in ribs of ice. Love still is Love;
His bow and arrows are the same: Great Julius,
That to his successors left the name of Cæsar,
Whom war could never tame, that with dry eyes
Beheld the large plains of Pharsalia cover'd
With the dead carcases of senators,
And citizens of Rome; when the world knew
No other lord but him, struck deep in years too,
(And men gray-hair'd forget the loves of youth,)
After all this, meeting fair Cleopatra,
A suppliant too, the magic of her eye,
Even in his pride of conquest, took him captive:
Nor are you more secure.

MAXIMINUS
Were you deform'd,
(But, by the gods, you are most excellent,)
Your gravity and discretion would o'ercome me;
And I should be more proud in being prisoner
To your fair virtues, than of all the honours,
Wealth, title, empire, that my sword hath purchased.

DIOCLESIAN
This meets my wishes. Welcome it, Artemia,
With outstretch'd arms, and study to forget
That Antoninus ever was: thy fate
Reserved thee for this better choice; embrace it.

MAXIMINUS
This happy match brings new nerves to give strength
To our continued league.

DIOCLESIAN
Hymen himself
Will bless this marriage, which we'll solemnize
In the presence of these kings.

KING of PONTUS
Who rest most happy,
To be eye-witnesses of a match that brings
Peace to the empire.

DIOCLESIAN
We much thank your loves:
But where's Sapritius, our governor,
And our most zealous provost, good Theophilus?

If ever prince were blest in a true servant,
Or could the gods be debtors to a man,
Both they and we stand far engaged to cherish
His piety and service.

ARTEMIA
Sir, the governor
Brooks sadly his son's loss, although he turn'd
Apostata in death; but bold Theophilus,
Who for the same cause, in my presence, seal'd
His holy anger on his daughters' hearts;
Having with tortures first tried to convert her,
Dragg'd the bewitching Christian to the scaffold,
And saw her lose her head.

DIOCLESIAN
He is all worthy:
And from his own mouth I would gladly hear
The manner how she suffer'd.

ARTEMIA
'Twill be deliver'd
With such contempt and scorn, (I know his nature,)
That rather 'twill beget your highness' laughter,
Than the least pity.

DIOCLESIAN
To that end I would hear it.

[Enter **THEOPHILUS, SAPRITIUS, and MACRINUS.**

ARTEMIA
He comes; with him the governor.

DIOCLESIAN
O, Sapritius,
I am to chide you for your tenderness;
But yet, remembering that you are a father,
I will forget it. Good Theophilus,
I'll speak with you anon.—Nearer, your ear.

[To **SAPRITIUS.**

THEOPHILUS [aside to **MACRINUS.**]
By Antoninus' soul, I do conjure you,
And though not for religion, for his friendship,
Without demanding what's the cause that moves me,
Receive my signet:—By the power of this,

Go to my prisons, and release all Christians,
That are in fetters there by my command.

MACRINUS
But what shall follow?

THEOPHILUS
Haste then to the port;
You there shall find two tall ships ready rigg'd,
In which embark the poor distressed souls,
And bear them from the reach of tyranny.
Enquire not whither you are bound: the Deity
That they adore will give you prosperous winds,
And make your voyage such, and largely pay for
Your hazard, and your travail. Leave me here;
There is a scene that I must act alone:
Haste, good Macrinus; and the great God guide you!

MACRINUS
I'll undertake 't; there's something prompts me to it;
'Tis to save innocent blood, a saint-like act:
And to be merciful has never been
By moral men themselves esteem'd a sin.

[Exit.

DIOCLESIAN
You know your charge?

SAPRITIUS
And will with care observe it.

DIOCLESIAN
For I profess he is not Cæsar's friend,
That sheds a tear for any torture that
A Christian suffers. Welcome, my best servant,
My careful, zealous provost! thou hast toil'd
To satisfy my will, though in extremes:
I love thee for 't; thou art firm rock, no changeling.
Prithee deliver, and for my sake do it,
Without excess of bitterness, or scoffs,
Before my brother and these kings, how took
The Christian her death?

THEOPHILUS
And such a presence,
Though every private head in this large room
Were circled round with an imperial crown,

Her story will deserve, it is so full
Of excellence and wonder.

DIOCLESIAN
Ha! how is this?

THEOPHILUS
O! mark it, therefore, and with that attention,
As you would hear an embassy from heaven
By a wing'd legate; for the truth deliver'd,
Both how, and what, this blessed virgin suffer'd,
And Dorothea but hereafter named,
You will rise up with reverence, and no more,
As things unworthy of your thoughts, remember
What the canonized Spartan ladies were,
Which lying Greece so boasts of. Your own matrons,
Your Roman dames, whose figures you yet keep
As holy relics, in her history
Will find a second urn: Gracchus' Cornelia,
Paulina, that in death desired to follow
Her husband Seneca, nor Brutus' Portia,
That swallow'd burning coals to overtake him,
Though all their several worths were given to one,
With this is to be mention'd.

MAXIMINUS
Is he mad?

DIOCLESIAN
Why, they did die, Theophilus, and boldly;
This did no more.

THEOPHILUS
They, out of desperation,
Or for vain glory of an after-name,
Parted with life: this had not mutinous sons,
As the rash Gracchi were; nor was this saint
A doting mother, as Cornelia was.
This lost no husband, in whose overthrow
Her wealth and honour sunk; no fear of want
Did make her being tedious; but, aiming
At an immortal crown, and in His cause
Who only can bestow it; who sent down
Legions of ministering angels to bear up
Her spotless soul to heaven, who entertain'd it
With choice celestial music, equal to
The motion of the spheres; she, uncompell'd,
Changed this life for a better. My lord Sapritius,

You were present at her death; did you e'er hear
Such ravishing sounds?

SAPRITIUS
Yet you said then 'twas witchcraft,
And devilish illusions.

THEOPHILUS
I then heard it
With sinful ears, and belch'd out blasphemous words
Against his Deity, which then I knew not,
Nor did believe in him.

DIOCLESIAN
Why, dost thou now?
Or dar'st thou, in our hearing—

THEOPHILUS
Were my voice
As loud as is His thunder, to be heard
Through all the world, all potentates on earth
Ready to burst with rage, should they but hear it;
Though hell, to aid their malice, lent her furies,
Yet I would speak, and speak again, and boldly:
I am a Christian; and the Powers you worship,
But dreams of fools and madmen.

MAXIMINUS
Lay hands on him.

DIOCLESIAN
Thou twice a child! for doting age so makes thee,
Thou couldst not else, thy pilgrimage of life
Being almost past through, in this last moment
Destroy whate'er thou hast done good or great—
Thy youth did promise much; and, grown a man,
Thou mad'st it good, and, with increase of years,
Thy actions still better'd: as the sun,
Thou didst rise gloriously, kept'st a constant course
In all thy journey; and now, in the evening,
When thou shouldst pass with honour to thy rest,
Wilt thou fall like a meteor?

SAPRITIUS
Yet confess
That thou art mad, and that thy tongue and heart
Had no agreement.

MAXIMINUS

Do; no way is left, else,
To save thy life, Theophilus.

DIOCLESIAN

But, refuse it,
Destruction as horrid, and as sudden,
Shall fall upon thee, as if hell stood open,
And thou wert sinking thither.

THEOPHILUS

Hear me, yet;
Hear, for my service past.

ARTEMIA

What will he say?

THEOPHILUS

As ever I deserved your favour, hear me,
And grant one boon; 'tis not for life I sue for;
Nor is it fit that I, that ne'er knew pity
To any Christian, being one myself,
Should look for any; no, I rather beg
The utmost of your cruelty. I stand
Accomptable for thousand Christians' deaths;
And, were it possible that I could die
A day for every one, then live again
To be again tormented, 'twere to me
An easy penance, and I should pass through
A gentle cleansing fire; but, that denied me,
It being beyond the strength of feeble nature,
My suit is, you would have no pity on me.
In mine own house there are a thousand engines
Of studied cruelty, which I did prepare
For miserable Christians; let me feel,
As the Sicilian did his brazen bull[1],
The horrid'st you can find; and I will say,
In death, that you are merciful.

DIOCLESIAN

Despair not;
In this thou shalt prevail. Go fetch them hither:

[Exit some of the **GUARD**.

Death shall put on a thousand shapes at once,
And so appear before thee; racks, and whips!—
Thy flesh, with burning pincers torn, shall feed

The fire that heats them; and what's wanting to
The torture of thy body, I'll supply
In punishing thy mind. Fetch all the Christians
That are in hold; and here, before his face,
Cut them in pieces.

THEOPHILUS
'Tis not in thy power:
It was the first good deed I ever did.
They are removed out of thy reach; howe'er,
I was determined for my sins to die,
I first took order for their liberty;
And still I dare thy worst.

[Re-enter **GUARD** with racks and other instruments of torture.

DIOCLESIAN
Bind him, I say;
Make every artery and sinew crack:
The slave that makes him give the loudest shriek,
Shall have ten thousand drachmas: wretch! I'll force thee
To curse the Power thou worship'st.

THEOPHILUS
Never, never:
No breath of mine shall e'er be spent on Him,

[They torment him.

But what shall speak His majesty or mercy.
I'm honour'd in my sufferings. Weak tormentors,
More tortures, more:—alas! you are unskilful—
For heaven's sake more; my breast is yet untorn:
Here purchase the reward that was propounded.
The irons cool,—here are arms yet, and thighs;
Spare no part of me.

MAXIMINUS
He endures beyond
The sufferance of a man.

SAPRITIUS
No sigh nor groan,
To witness he hath feeling.

DIOCLESIAN
Harder, villains!

[Enter **HARPAX**.

HARPAX
Unless that he blaspheme, he's lost for ever.
If torments ever could bring forth despair,
Let these compel him to it:—Oh me!
My ancient enemies again!

[Falls down.

[Enter **DOROTHEA** in a white robe, a crown upon her head, led in by **ANGELO; ANTONINUS, CALISTA,**
and **CHRISTETA** following, all in white, but less glorious; **ANGELO** holds out a crown to **THEOPHILUS.**

THEOPHILUS
Most glorious vision!—
Did e'er so hard a bed yield man a dream
So heavenly as this? I am confirm'd,
Confirm'd, you blessed spirits, and make haste
To take that crown of immortality
You offer to me. Death! till this blest minute,
I never thought thee slow-paced; nor would I
Hasten thee now, for any pain I suffer,
But that thou keep'st me from a glorious wreath,
Which through this stormy way I would creep to,
And, humbly kneeling, with humility wear it.
Oh! now I feel thee:—blessed spirits! I come;
And, witness for me all these wounds and scars,
I die a soldier in the Christian wars.

[Dies.

SAPRITIUS
I have seen thousands tortured, but ne'er yet
A constancy like this.

HARPAX
I am twice damn'd.

ANGELO
Haste to thy place appointed, cursed fiend!

[**HARPAX** sinks with thunder and lightning.

In spite of hell, this soldier's not thy prey;
'Tis I have won, thou that hast lost the day.

[Exit with **DOROTHEA** &c.

DIOCLESIAN
I think the centre of the earth be crack'd—
Yet I stand still unmoved, and will go on:
The persecution that is here begun,
Through all the world with violence shall run.

[Flourish.

[Exeunt.

FOOTNOTE

[1] As the Sicilian did his brazen bull.] The brazen bull, an ingenious instrument of torture, invented by Perillus, and presented to Phalaris, the tyrant of Agrigentum, was fatal both to its author and its owner. Phalaris made the first experiment of its powers upon Perillus; and when the people, exasperated by his cruelties, eventually rose against him, the tyrant suffered death by its means himself.

PHILIP MASSINGER – A SHORT BIOGRAPHY

Very few materials exist for a life of Massinger beyond the entries of the Parish Register or the College Books, and a few slender intimations scattered here and there in the dedications to his plays. From these scanty sources the following brief memoir is derived.

Our author was born at Salisbury[1] in the year 1584: he was the son of Arthur Massinger, a gentleman in the service of Henry, the second Earl of Pembroke[2]. We must not suppose, from his being thus attached to the family of a nobleman, that the father of our poet was a person of inferior birth and station. In those days the word servant carried with it no sense of degradation. The great lords and officers of the court numbered inferior nobles among their followers. We read, in Cavendish's Life of Wolsey, that "my Lord Percy, the son and heir of the Earl of Northumberland, attended upon and was servitor to the lord-cardinal[3]:" and from the situation which Arthur Massinger held in the household of so high and influential a person as the Earl of Pembroke, we might be justly led to argue rather favourably than unfavourably of his family and his connexions. "There were," says Mr. Gifford, "many considerations which united to render this state of dependance respectable and even honourable. The secretaries, clerks, and assistants, of various departments, were not then, as now, nominated by the government, but left to the choice of the person who held the employment; and as no particular dwelling was officially set apart for their residence, they were entertained in the house of their principal. That communication, too, between noblemen of power and trust, both of a public and private nature, which is now committed to the post, was in those days managed by confidential servants, who were despatched from one to the other, and even to the sovereign[4];" and, indeed, the father of our poet himself was, we know, in one instance thus employed as the bearer of communications from his patron to Elizabeth. We read in The Sidney Letters[5], "Mr. Massinger is newly come up from the Earl of Pembroke with letters to the queen for his lordship's leave to be away this St. George's Day." This was an errand which would not have been intrusted to the execution of any inconsiderable person: unimportant as the occasion may appear to us, it would not have been regarded in that light by

Elizabeth; for no monarch ever exacted from the nobility, and particularly from her officers of state, a more rigid and scrupulous compliance with stated order than this princess.

With regard to the early youth of Massinger, we possess no information whatever. Mr. Gifford supposes that it might have been passed at Wilton, a seat belonging to the Earl of Pembroke, in the neighbourhood of Salisbury; but this mode of disposing of his early years rests on a very improbable conjecture. It may occasionally have happened that the child of a favourite dependant was admitted as the companion of the younger branches of the patron's family, and allowed to receive his education among them; but this was certainly not an ordinary case; and, like Cavendish, a large majority of the great man's servants and dependants "left wife and children, home and family, rest and quietness, only to serve him[6]."—Massinger was most likely educated at the grammar-school of Salisbury, where many distinguished characters have received the rudiments of their education, among whom the elegant and accomplished Addison is to be numbered. But wherever the first years of our poet's life may have been spent, and whatever may have been the nature of his education, we know that at the age of eighteen (May 14, 1602) he was entered at the university of Oxford, and became a commoner of St. Alban's Hall[7].

Massinger resided at Oxford about four years, and then abruptly left it, without taking any degree. The cause of this sudden departure is ascribed by Mr. Gifford to the death of his father, from whom his supplies were derived: but Davies relates a very different story, and asserts that the Earl of Pembroke, who had sent him to the university and maintained him there, withdrew the necessary allowance in consequence of his having misapplied the time demanded for severer studies, in the pursuit of a more attractive but less profitable description of literature. Each opinion is equally ungrounded on the basis of any substantial evidence, and rests almost entirely on the imagination of the biographer: what slight authority there is favours the latter supposition, which, perhaps, on the whole, is most consistent with the known circumstances of the case. Anthony Wood, who was born, lived, and died at Oxford; who spent his time in collecting and recording the gossip which circulated in the university respecting the characters and conduct of its more distinguished sons; and whose evidence, however indifferent it may be, is the best that can be obtained upon the subject, confirms the representation of Davies:— "Massinger," says Wood, "gave his mind more to poetry and romance, for about four years or more, than to logic and philosophy, which he ought to have done, as he was patronised to that end." This passage corroborates the account of Davies so far as to intimate that patronage was afforded to our author, and that cause of dissatisfaction was given to the patron; but it goes no farther: it does not even state to whom the poet was indebted for assistance, nor that the misapplication of his academic hours was at all resented by the friend from whom the assistance was received: but still Wood is very probably correct in his information that other than his paternal funds were depended upon for maintaining Massinger at the university; and if such was the case, there can be no question from whose hands they must have proceeded; while the simple fact of his having been totally neglected, from the time of his father's death, by the whole of the Pembroke family, till after the demise of the earl, carries with it a strong suspicion that some offence was committed on the side of the poet, and tenaciously remembered on the side of the peer. Henry, the second Earl of Pembroke, died (1601) the year before Massinger was admitted at Oxford; and William, the third earl, to whom the father of Massinger continued attached during life, is universally and justly considered one of the brightest ornaments of the courts of Elizabeth and James. He was a man of generous and liberal disposition; the distinguished patron of arts and learning; and a lover of poetry, which he himself cultivated with some degree of success. It is not probable—it is impossible—that such a man should have allowed the highly talented son of an old and faithful servant of his family to be checked in his course of study, and abandoned to maintain, through the early years of life, a single-handed contest with adversity, for the want of that pecuniary aid which he could have yielded and never missed, unless some strong and decided cause of displeasure had existed. Had Massinger been merely forced to leave the university, as Mr. Gifford supposes, because the funds necessary to maintain him there had failed with the life of his father, we impute an act of illiberality to the Earl of Pembroke which is inconsistent with the whole tenor of his life and character. From whatever source the expenses of our author's education were originally defrayed, their suddenly ceasing argues in favour of the account intimated by Wood and detailed by Davies. If his father had, during his life, supported him at the university, there must have been some reason for the earl's not continuing that support when the father of Massinger was no more; and perhaps the most honourable supposition for both parties is that which represents the earl as offended by the bent of our author's studies and pursuits. By adopting this view of the case we are saved from the painful necessity of either assuming, on the one hand, that a nobleman distinguished among the most amiable characters of his age allowed a highly gifted and meritorious young man, a natural dependant of his house, to languish in the want of that countenance and protection on which he had an hereditary claim; or, on the other hand, that Massinger had incurred the displeasure of his natural and hereditary patron by the commission of some more crying offence.

Every, even the slightest, surmise of Mr. Gifford is deserving attention and respect; but I cannot admit the supposition by which he would account for the alienation that subsisted between the Earl of Pembroke and our author. That distinguished critic has inferred, from the religious sentiments contained in The Virgin Martyr, that Massinger was a Roman catholic, and for that cause neglected by the protector of his father. But if the intimations scattered through this play and others should be received as sufficient evidence of the faith of Massinger, we must, on similar evidence—the intimations contained in Measure for Measure, for instance—conclude that the religion of Shakspeare was the same; and then we are cast back upon our old difficulty, and have to explain why William Earl of Pembroke, a celebrated patron of literary men, and of dramatists in particular, scorned to yield his notice to the catholic Massinger, while (to use the expression of Heminge and Condell) he "prosequuted" the catholic Shakspeare and "his works with so much favour[8]?" There are many reasons for believing Shakspeare to have been a member of the church of Rome; and the patronage afforded him by the Earl of Pembroke proves, that that nobleman extended his liberality to men of genius without any regard to distinctions of faith; but, on the other hand, we have no just grounds for assuming that Massinger really did hold the same opinions. The only evidence we have upon this point, that afforded by the general tone of his writings, is of a most vague and superficial description. What, in fact, can be inferred from it? We may from such a source derive very satisfactory information respecting the sentiments which would be favourably received by the audience, but very little respecting those of the author. The truth is, that though the national religion was reformed in its liturgy and articles, the feelings, prejudices, and superstitions of the people were still almost entirely catholic; and Massinger, like any other dramatic author, writing for the amusement of the people, necessarily addressed them in a language they would understand, and with sentiments that accorded with their own. Besides, as a poet, he would never carry his theological distinctions to his literary labours: Voltaire himself is catholic in his tragedies; and Massinger naturally adopted the creed which was most suitable to the purposes of poetry, and afforded the most picturesque ceremonies and romantic situations. I feel inclined, therefore, to dismiss entirely the theory suggested by Mr. Gifford, for these two reasons; first, supposing our author to have been a catholic, we have no reason for condemning the Earl of Pembroke as a bigot and a persecutor, who would close his eyes to the merits of so great an author, because his faith did not tally with his own; and, secondly, we have no sufficient grounds for supposing him to have been a catholic at all. But with regard to all such visionary conjectures, thinking is literally a waste of thought.

Whatever may have been the nature of Massinger's studies at Oxford, it is quite certain, from the general character of his works, that his time could not have been wasted there; and his literary acquirements, at the period of his leaving the university, appear to have been multifarious and extensive. He was about two-and-twenty (1606) when he arrived in London, where, as he more than once observes, he was driven by his necessities, and somewhat inclined, perhaps, by the peculiar bent of his talents, to dedicate himself to the service of the stage.

The theatre, when Massinger first took up his abode in the metropolis, must have presented attractions of all others the most calculated to excite the interest, and inspire the imagination, of a young man of sensibility, taste, and education like our poet. No art ever attained a more rapid maturity than the dramatic art in England. The people had, indeed, been long accustomed to a species of exhibition, called MIRACLES or MYSTERIES, founded on sacred subjects, and performed by the ministers of religion themselves, on the holy festivals, in or near the churches, and designed to instruct the ignorant in the leading facts of sacred history[9]. From the occasional introduction of allegorical characters, such as Faith, Death, Hope, or Sin, into these religious dramas, representations of another kind, called MORALITIES, had by degrees arisen, of which the plots were more artificial, regular, and connected, and which were entirely formed of such personifications: but the first rough draught of a regular tragedy and comedy—Lord Sackville's Gorboduc, and Still's Gammer Gurton's Needle[10]—were not produced till within the latter half of the sixteenth century, and little more than twenty years before the stage acquired its highest splendour in the productions of Shakspeare.

About the end of the sixteenth century, the attention of the public began to be more generally directed to the drama; and it throve most admirably beneath the cheering beams of popular favour. The theatrical performances which in the early part of Elizabeth's reign had been exhibited on temporary stages, erected in such halls or apartments as the actors could procure, or, more generally, in the yards of the larger inns, while the spectators surveyed them from the surrounding windows and galleries, began to find more convenient and permanent habitations. About the year 1569, a regular playhouse, under the appropriate name of The Theatre, was erected. It is supposed to have stood somewhere in Blackfriars; and, three years after the commencement of this establishment, the queen, yielding to her own inclination for such amusements, and disregarding the remonstrances of the Puritans, granted licence and authority to the servants of the Earl of Leicester ("for the recreation of her loving subjects, as for her own solace and pleasure when she should think good to see them") to exercise their occupation throughout the whole realm of England. From this time the number of theatres increased with the increasing demands of the people. Various noblemen had their respective companies of performers, who were associated as their servants, and acted under their protection; and when Massinger left Oxford, and commenced dramatic author, there were no less than seven principal theatres open in the metropolis.

With respect to the interior arrangements, there were very few points of difference between our modern theatres and those of the days of Massinger. The prices of admission, indeed, were considerably cheaper: to the boxes the entrance was a shilling; to the pit and galleries only sixpence. Sixpence also was the price paid for stools upon the stage; and these seats, as we learn from Decker's Gull's Hornbook, were particularly affected by the wits and critics of the time. The conduct of the audience was less restrained by the sense of public decorum, and smoking tobacco, playing at cards, eating and drinking, were generally prevalent among them. The hours of performance were also earlier: the play commencing at one o'clock. During the representation a flag was unfurled at the top of the theatre; and the stage, according to the universal practice of the age, was strewn with rushes; but, in all other respects, the theatres of Elizabeth and James's days seem to have borne a perfect resemblance to our own. They had their pit, where the inferior class of spectators, the groundlings, vented their clamorous censure or approbation; they had their boxes—rooms as they were called—to which the right of exclusive admission was engaged by the night, for the more affluent portion of the audience; and there were again the galleries, or scaffoldings above the boxes, for those who were content to purchase less commodious situations at a cheaper rate. On the stage, in the same manner, the appointments appear to have been nearly of the same description as at present. The curtain divided the audience from the actors, which, at the third sounding, not indeed of the bell, but of the trumpet, was drawn for the commencement of the performance. Malone, in his account of the ancient theatre, supposes that there were no moveable scenes; that a permanent elevation of about nine feet was raised at the back of the stage, from which, in many of the old plays, part of the dialogue was spoken; and that there was a private box on each side this platform. Such an arrangement would have destroyed all theatrical illusion; and it seems extraordinary that any spectators should desire to fix themselves in a station where they could have seen nothing but the backs and trains of the performers; but, as Malone himself acknowledges the spot to have been inconvenient, and that "it is not very easy to ascertain the precise situation where these boxes really were[11]", it may very reasonably be presumed, that they were not placed in the position that the historian of the English stage has supposed. As to the permanent floor, or upper stage, of which he speaks, he may or may not be correct in his statement. All that his quotations upon the subject really establish is, that in the old, as in the modern theatre, when the actor was to speak from a window, or balcony, or the walls of a fortress, the requisite ingenuity was not wanting to contrive a representation of the place. But with regard to the use of painted moveable scenery, it is not possible, from the very circumstances of the case, to believe him correct in his theory. Such a contrivance could not have escaped our ancestors. All the materials were ready to their hands. They had not to invent for themselves, but merely to adapt an old invention to that peculiar purpose; and at a time when every better-furnished apartment was adorned with tapestry; when even the rooms of the commonest taverns were hung with painted cloths; while all the materials were constantly before their eyes, we can hardly believe our forefathers to have been so deficient in ingenuity, as to have missed the simple contrivance of converting the common ornaments of their walls into the decorations of their theatres. But, in fact, the use of scenery was almost co-existent with the introduction of dramatic representations in this country. In the Chester Mysteries (1268), the most ancient and complete collection of the kind which we possess, is found the following stage direction: "Then Noe shall go into the arke with all his familye, his wife excepte. The arke must be boarded round about; and upon the boardes all the beastes and fowles, hereafter rehearsed, must be painted, that their wordes may agree with their pictures[12]." In this passage we have a clear reference to a painted scene. It is not likely that, in the lapse of three centuries, while all other arts were in a state of rapid improvement, and the art of dramatic writing, perhaps, more rapidly and successfully improved than any other, the art of theatrical decoration should have alone stood still. It is not improbable that their scenes were few; and that they were varied, as occasion might require, by the introduction of different pieces of stage furniture. Mr. Gifford, who adheres to the opinions of Malone, says, "A table with a pen and ink thrust in, signified that the stage was a counting-house; if these were withdrawn and two stools put in their place, it was then a tavern[13]." And this might be perfectly satisfactory as long as the business of the play was supposed to be passing within doors; but when it was removed to the open air, such meagre devices would no longer be sufficient to guide the imagination of the audience, and some new method must have been adopted to indicate the place of action. After giving the subject very considerable attention, I cannot help thinking that Steevens was right in rejecting Malone's theory, and concluding that the spectators were, as at the present day, assisted in following the progress of the story by means of painted moveable scenery. This opinion is confirmed by the ancient stage directions. In the folio Shakspeare, 1623, we read "Enter Brutus in his orchard; Enter Timon in the woods; Enter Timon from the cave." In Coriolanus, "Marcius follows them to the gates and is shut in." Innumerable instances of the same kind might be cited to prove that the ancient stage was not so defective in the necessary decorations as some antiquaries of great authority would represent. "It may be added," says Steevens, "that the dialogue of our old dramatists has such perpetual reference to objects supposed visible to the audience, that the want of scenery could not have failed to render many of the descriptions absurd. Banquo examines the outside of Inverness castle with such minuteness, that he distinguishes even the nests which the martens had built under the projecting part of its roof. Romeo, standing in a garden, points to the tops of fruit-trees gilded by the moon. The prologue speaker to the second part of Henry the Fourth expressly shows the spectators 'This worm-eaten hold of ragged stone,' in which Northumberland was lodged. Iachimo takes the most exact inventory of every article in Imogen's bed-chamber, from the silk and silver of which her tapestry was wrought, down to the Cupids that support her andirons. Had not the inside of the apartment, with its proper furniture, been represented, how ridiculous must the action of Iachimo have appeared! He must have stood looking out of the room for the particulars supposed to be visible within it." The works of Massinger would afford innumerable instances of a similar kind to vindicate the opinion which Steevens has asserted on the testimony of Shakspeare alone. But on this subject there is one passage which appears to me quite conclusive. Must not all the humour of the mock play in The Midsummer Night's Dream have been entirely lost, unless the audience before whom it was performed were accustomed to all the embellishments requisite to give effect to a dramatic representation, and could consequently estimate the absurdity of those shallow contrivances and mean substitutes for scenery devised by the ignorance of the clowns[14]?

In only one respect do I perceive any material difference between the mode of representation at the time of Massinger and at present: in his day, the female parts were performed by boys. This custom, which must in many cases have materially injured the illusion of the scene, was in others of considerable advantage: it furnished the stage with a succession of youths, regularly educated for the art, to fill, in every department of the drama, the characters suited to their age. When the lad had become too tall for Juliet, he had acquired the skill, and was most admirably fitted, both in age and appearance, for performing the part which Garrick considered the most difficult on the stage, because it needed "an old head upon young shoulders," the ardent and arduous character of Romeo. When the voice had "the mannish crack," that rendered the youth unfit to appear as the representative of the gentle Imogen, the stage possessed in him the very person that was wanting to do justice to the princely sentiments of Arviragus or Guiderius[15].

Such was the state of the stage when Massinger arrived in the metropolis, and dedicated his talents to its service. He joined a splendid fraternity, for Shakspeare, Jonson, Beaumont, Fletcher, Shirley, were then flourishing at the height of their reputation, and the full vigour of their genius. Massinger came among them no unworthy competitor for such honours and emoluments as the theatre could afford. Of the honours, indeed, he seems to have reaped a very fair and equitable portion; of the emoluments, the harvest was less abundant. In those days, very little pecuniary reward was to be gained by the dramatic poet, unless, as indeed was most frequently the case, he added the profession of the actor to that of the author, and recited the verses which he wrote. The distinguished performers of that time, Alleyn, Burbage, Heminge, Condell, Shakspeare, all appear to have died in independent, if not affluent, circumstances; but the remuneration obtained by the poet was most miserably curtailed. The price given at the theatre for a new play fluctuated between ten and twenty pounds; the copyright, if the piece was printed, might produce from six to ten pounds more; in addition to these sums, the dedication-fee may be reckoned, the usual amount of which was forty shillings. Our author appears to have produced about two or three plays every year. Most of them were successful; but, even with this industry and good fortune, his annual income would rarely have exceeded fifty pounds: and we cannot, therefore, feel surprised at finding him continually speaking of his necessities; or that the only existing document connected with his life should be one that represents him in a state of pecuniary embarrassment.

Among the papers of Dulwich College, the indefatigable Mr. Malone discovered the following letter tripartite, which, coming from persons of such deserved celebrity, cannot fail of interesting the reader.

"To our most loving friend, Mr. Phillip Hinchlow, esquire, these.

"Mr. Hinchlow,

"You understand our unfortunate extremitie, and I doe not thincke you so void of Christianitie but that you would throw so much money into the Thames as wee request now of you, rather than endanger so many innocent lives. You know there is xl. more, at least, to be receaved of you for the play. We desire you to lend us vl. of that, which shall be allowed to you; without which, we cannot be bayled, nor I play any more till this be dispatch'd. It will lose you xxl. ere the end of the next weeke, besides the hindrance of the next new play. Pray, sir, consider our cases with humanity, and now give us cause to acknowledge you our true freind in time of neede. Wee have entreated Mr. Davison to deliver this note, as well to witness your love as our promises, and alwayes acknowledgement to be ever

"Your most thankfull and loving friends,
"NAT. FIELD[16]."

"The money shall be abated out of the money remayns for the play of Mr. Fletcher and ours.
"ROB. DABORNE[17]."

"I have ever found you a true loving friend to mee, and in soe small a suite, it beinge honest, I hope you will not fail us.
"PHILIP MASSINGER."

Indorsed.
"Received by mee, Robert Davison, of Mr. Hinchlow, for the use of Mr. Daboerne, Mr. Feeld, Mr. Messenger, the sum of vl.
"ROB. DAVISON[18]."

The occasion of the distress in which these three distinguished persons were involved it is not possible to fathom. We may imagine a thousand emergencies, either creditable or discreditable to the fame of the writers, with which the letter would perfectly tally; but, on such slight and vague intimations, no ingenuity could determine which was most likely to be correct. But from the document a circumstance is ascertained, which, before its discovery, had been called in question. Sir Aston Cockayne, a friend of Massinger, had asserted in a volume of poems, published in 1658, that our author had written in conjunction with Fletcher; Davies doubted this report, but the above letter establishes the fact beyond the possibility of dispute.

Massinger is known to have produced thirty-seven plays for the stage, a list of which is given at the conclusion of this memoir. Sixteen entire plays and the fragment of another, The Parliament of Love, alone are extant. No less than eleven of his productions, in manuscript, were in possession of Mr. Warburton (Somerset Herald), and destroyed with the rest of that gentleman's invaluable collection by his cook, who, ignorant of their worth, used them as waste paper for the purposes of the kitchen.

The great and various merits of the works of Massinger will be better seen in the following volumes than in any elaborate, critical dissertation. If our author be compared with the other dramatic writers of his age, we cannot long hesitate where to place him. More natural in his characters and more poetical in his diction than Jonson or Cartwright, more elevated and nervous than Fletcher, the only writers who can be supposed to contest his pre-eminence, Massinger ranks immediately under Shakspeare himself. Our poet excels, perhaps, more in the description than in the expression of passion; this may in some measure be ascribed to his attention to the fable: while his scenes are managed with consummate skill, the lighter shades of character and sentiment are lost in the tendency of each part to the catastrophe. The melody, force, and variety of his versification are always remarkable. The prevailing beauties of his productions are dignity and elegance; their predominant fault is want of passion.

Massinger's last play—which is unfortunately lost—The Anchoress of Pausilippo, was acted Jan. 26, 1640, about six weeks before his death, which happened on the 17th of March, 1640. He went to bed in good health, says Langbaine, and was found dead in the morning, in his own house on the Bankside. He was buried in the churchyard of St. Saviour's, and the comedians paid the last sad duty to his name, by attending him to the grave.

It does not appear, though every stone and every fragment of a stone has been carefully examined, that any monument or inscription of any kind marked the place where his dust was deposited. "The memorial of his mortality," says Gifford, "is given with a pathetic brevity, which accords but too well with the obscure and humble passages of his life: March 20, 1639-40, buried Philip Massinger, A STRANGER."

Such is all the information that remains to us of this distinguished poet. But though we are ignorant of every circumstance respecting him but that he lived, wrote, and died, we may yet form some idea of his personal character from the recommendatory poems prefixed to his several plays, in which, as Mr. Gifford justly observes, the language of his panegyrists, though warm, expresses an attachment apparently derived not so much from his talents as his virtues: he is their beloved, much-esteemed, dear, worthy, deserving, honoured, long-known, and long-loved friend. All the writers of his life represent him as a man of singular modesty, gentleness, candour, and affability; nor does it appear that he ever made or found an enemy.

FOOTNOTES:

[1] *The register of his birth is not to be found, but all writers of his life agree in naming this city as the place of his nativity; and their account is corroborated by the college entry, which styles him Salisburiensis.*

[2] *Dedication to The Bondman.*

[3] *Singer's edition, p. 120.*

[4] *Introduction to the Works of Massinger, p. xxxviii.*

[5] *Vol. ii. p. 933.*

[6] *Life of Wolsey, p. 517.*

[7] *The entry in the college book styles him "Phillip Massinger, Salisburiensis, generosi filius."*

[8] *Dedication to the folio edition of Shakspeare.*

[9] *Indulgences were granted to those who attended the representation of them.*

[10] *Gorboduc appeared in 1562; Gammer Gurton, in 1566.*

[11] *Reed's Shakspeare, vol. iii. p. 83, note 3.*

[12] *Reed's Shakspeare, vol. iii. p. 15.*

[13] *Gifford's Massinger, vol. i. p. 103.*

[14] *This question ought to be set at rest, methinks, by the following extract from the Book of Revels, the oldest that exists, in the office of the auditors of the imprest: "Mrs. Dane, the lynnen dealer, for canvass to paynte for houses for the players, and other properties, as monsters, great hollow trees, and such other, twenty dozen ells, 12l."—See Boswell's Shakspeare, vol. iii. p. 364, et seq.*

[15] *The first woman who appeared in a regular drama, on a public stage, played Desdemona, about the year 1660. Her name is unknown.*

[16] *Nat. Field. This celebrated actor played female parts. He was the author of two comedies: A Woman's a Weathercock, 1612, and Amends for Ladies, 1618. He also assisted Massinger in The Fatal Dowry.*

[17] *Robert Daborne was the author of two plays: The Christian turned Turk, 1612, and The poor Man's Comfort, 1655. He was a gentleman of liberal education, master of arts, and in holy orders. It is supposed that he had preferment in Ireland. A sermon by him, preached at Waterford, in 1618, is extant.*

[18] *Additions to Malone's Hist. Account of Eng. Stage, p. 488.*

PHILIP MASSINGER – A CONCISE BIBLIOGRAPHY

As would be expected many works from this time not longer exist either in part or their entirety. Further many playwrights collaborated on plays or revised them for later performances and we have used the latest position known on each of them for the bibliography below..

Solo Plays
The Maid of Honour, tragicomedy (c. 1621; printed 1632)
The Duke of Milan, tragedy (c. 1621–3; printed 1623, 1638)
The Unnatural Combat, tragedy (c. 1621–6; printed 1639)
The Bondman, tragicomedy (licensed 3 December 1623; printed 1624)
The Renegado, tragicomedy (licensed 17 April 1624; printed 1630)

The Parliament of Love, comedy (licensed 3 November 1624; MS)
A New Way to Pay Old Debts, comedy (c. 1625; printed 1632)
The Roman Actor, tragedy (licensed 11 October 1626; printed 1629)
The Great Duke of Florence, tragicomedy (licensed 5 July 1627; printed 1636)
The Picture, tragicomedy (licensed 8 June 1629; printed 1630)
The Emperor of the East, tragicomedy (licensed 11 March 1631; printed 1632)
Believe as You List, tragedy (rejected by the censor in January, but licensed 6 May 1631; MS)
The City Madam, comedy (licensed 25 May 1632; printed 1658)
The Guardian, comedy (licensed 31 October 1633; printed 1655)
The Bashful Lover, tragicomedy (licensed 9 May 1636; printed 1655)

Collaborations with John Fletcher
Sir John van Olden Barnavelt, tragedy (August 1619; MS)
The Little French Lawyer, comedy (c. 1619–23; printed 1647)
A Very Woman, tragicomedy (c. 1619–22; licensed 6 June 1634; printed 1655)
The Custom of the Country, comedy (c. 1619–23; printed 1647)
The Double Marriage, tragedy (c. 1619–23; Printed 1647)
The False One, history (c. 1619–23; printed 1647)
The Prophetess, tragicomedy (licensed 14 May 1622; printed 1647)
The Sea Voyage, comedy (licensed 22 June 1622; printed 1647)
The Spanish Curate, comedy (licensed 24 October 1622; printed 1647)
The Lovers' Progress or The Wandering Lovers, tragicomedy (licensed 6 Dec 1623; rev 1634; printed 1647)
The Elder Brother, comedy (c. 1625; printed 1637).

Collaborations with John Fletcher and Francis Beaumont
Thierry and Theodoret, tragedy (c. 1607?; printed 1621)
The Coxcomb, comedy (1608–10; printed 1647)
Beggars' Bush, comedy (c. 1612–15?; revised 1622?; printed 1647)
Love's Cure, comedy (c. 1612–15?; revised 1625?; printed 1647).

Collaborations with John Fletcher and Nathan Field
The Honest Man's Fortune, tragicomedy (1613; printed 1647)
The Queen of Corinth, tragicomedy (c. 1616–18; printed 1647)
The Knight of Malta, tragicomedy (c. 1619; printed 1647).

Collaborations with Nathan Field
The Fatal Dowry, tragedy (c. 1619, printed 1632); adapted by Nicholas Rowe: The Fair Penitent

Collaborations with John Fletcher, John Ford, and William Rowley, or John Webster
The Fair Maid of the Inn, comedy (licensed 22 January 1626; printed 1647).

Collaborations with John Fletcher, Ben Jonson, and George Chapman

Rollo Duke of Normandy, or The Bloody Brother, tragedy (c. 1616–24; printed 1639).

Collaborations with Thomas Dekker:
The Virgin Martyr, tragedy (licensed 6 October 1620; printed 1622).

Collaborations with Thomas Middleton and William Rowley:
The Old Law, comedy (c. 1615–18; printed 1656).

www.ingramcontent.com/pod-product-compliance
Lightning Source LLC
Chambersburg PA
CBHW060136050426
42448CB00010B/2158